JOURNEY TO
THE LAND OF
PROMISE

GENESIS–DEUTERONOMY

Journey to the Land of Promise
Genesis–Deuteronomy

Page H. Kelley

SMYTH & HELWYS
PUBLISHING, INC.
MACON, GEORGIA

ISBN 1-57312-160-6

Journey to the Land of Promise
Genesis–Deuteronomy

Page H. Kelley

Smyth & Helwys Publishing, Inc.
6316 Peake Road
Macon, Georgia 31210-3960
1-800-747-3016

Library of Congress Cataloging-in-Publication

Kelley, Page H.
    Journey to the land of promise: Genesis–Deuteronomy/
    Page H. Kelley.
    p. cm.
    Includes bibliographical references.
    ISBN 1-57312-160-6   (alk. paper)
    1. Bible. O.T. Pentateuch—Criticism, interpretation, etc.
    I. Title.
    BS1225.K39   1997
    222'.1061—dc21   97-19982
                                                                    CIP

Contents

Introduction

The Pentateuch

Why should anyone bother studying the Bible? Wouldn't it be better just to read it devotionally, leaving aside all so-called "helps" to Bible study? Aren't these helps limited in their usefulness by the limited knowledge and preconceived notions of their authors? Isn't the Bible alone a sufficient guide in matters of faith, doctrine, and Christian ethics?

I certainly would not want to detract from the importance of the devotional reading of the Bible. For those who take their faith seriously, there can be no substitute. Regular Bible reading undertaken in a context of prayer and meditation yields a rich harvest of spiritual benefits. In fact, this was the only way I knew how to read the Bible until I graduated from high school. What I learned in this way was sufficient to enable me to experience salvation through Jesus Christ and to begin to walk in the path of Christian discipleship.

Then, at the age of eighteen, my situation changed. Having responded to a call to the ministry, I enrolled in a Baptist college. I thus began what eventually proved to be a ten-year program of preparation including both college and seminary. Entering upon this new phase of my life caused me to examine the adequacy of my concept of the Bible and my approach to its study. At first I was somewhat hesitant to experiment with other approaches. I feared that perhaps I might lose more than I would gain in the process.

I soon discovered, however, that my fears were largely unfounded. I did not have to give up my devotional reading of the Bible. On the contrary, I found that it became more meaningful when supplemented and enriched by other approaches. The end result was that the Bible began to communicate with me on a much deeper level. That was more than a half century ago and the study of the Bible continues to be one of the top priorities of my life. I feel I can never learn enough from devoted scholars who have made it their life's business to open up the meaning of the Scriptures to others.

Importance

The first five books of the Bible are commonly referred to as the Pentateuch, a term indicating a scroll made up of five books. Jewish scholars, however, refer to these books by the Hebrew term "Torah." Torah has been traditionally translated as "Law," but this translation

is only partially correct. While the Pentateuch does include large
blocks of legal materials, it also contains a wide variety of other materials such as stories, genealogical lists, poetry, visions, dreams, and so
on. Genesis, for example, is made up entirely of nonlegal materials.
Even the book of Exodus, which records the giving of the Torah at
Sinai, contains very little legal material before chapter 20. The only
book composed almost entirely of legal matters is Leviticus.

A more accurate translation of Torah as a description of the
contents of the Pentateuch, therefore, would be "teaching,"
"guidance," "instruction," or "revelation."

It would be difficult to overemphasize the importance of the
Pentateuch for the rest of the Bible. Jewish scholars have long assigned
a place of preeminence among the books of the Hebrew Scriptures to
the Pentateuch. Ancient rabbis were fond of saying that it was the
heart and soul of the Hebrew Bible and that all the rest was merely
commentary.

The New Testament is no less dependent upon the Pentateuch.
Think of the revisions the New Testament would have to undergo if
the world had never heard of such persons as Adam and Eve, Noah,
Abraham and Sarah, or Moses and Aaron. What if the Hebrew
Scriptures made no mention of the garden of Eden, the flood, or the
exodus out of Egypt? Much of the Bible would be unintelligible
without this inspired beginning.

Contents

The Pentateuch opens with a brief account of events from Adam to
Abraham. It tells how God created the heavens and the earth and all
living creatures upon the earth. It recounts how the first human beings
rebelled against their Creator and were cast out of the garden of Eden.
It tells how the continuing rebellion of their offspring produced a
world so corrupt that God resolved to send a flood to wipe it out,
sparing only Noah and his family. The human race did no better after
the flood. Each new beginning led to more rebellion and disaster. This
time it happened on the plains of Shinar. The attempt of the people to
build a city and a tower whose top would reach to heaven caused them
to be scattered over the face of the earth and to be unable to communicate with each other due to the confusion of their languages.

Instead of abandoning the scattered nations to their fate, however,
God called Abraham to father a new nation and to become a kind of
"pilot project" in the redemption of all other nations. The remainder
of Genesis traces the wanderings of Abraham and his descendants,
who throughout their lifetime continued to be little more than

"sojourners in the land of promise." In the end, famine forced them to abandon the promised land and to seek food and shelter in Egypt.

In time they experienced an accelerated birth rate in their host country, and their numbers began to multiply. This led the Egyptians to fear them and eventually to enslave them. Their enslavement set the stage for the call of Moses and the miraculous exodus of the Israelites out of Egypt. Israel's Creator thus became its Liberator. The account of the exodus highlights God's dual control over the events of history and over the forces of nature.

The sequel to Israel's escape from Egypt was the covenant-making ceremony at Sinai (also known as Horeb, or the Mountain of God). Moses played a leading role in all these events. Shuttling up and down the mountain, he served as mediator between the people and God and brought down the tablets of the Law for their guidance.

The rest of the Pentateuch involves the building of the tabernacle, the further revelation of the Law to Moses, and the long and tortuous journey from Sinai to the borders of the promised land. Having finally arrived opposite the land, the people assembled to hear Moses reinterpret the Law and speak words of farewell before his death. The generation that heard the Law at Sinai had died in the wilderness, and a new generation, born in the wilderness, needed to be instructed in the ways of the Lord. Deuteronomy became the new message for a new day and continued to function in this role throughout Israelite history.

The overall sweep of the materials included in the Pentateuch can be seen in the following outline:

    I. From Creation to Abraham (Gen 1–11)
    II. Abraham's Pilgrimage of Faith (Gen 12–25)
    III. Heirs of the Promise: Isaac, Jacob, and Joseph (Gen 26–50)
    IV. From Egypt to Sinai (Exod 1–18)
    V. Covenant and Law at Sinai (Exod 19–40)
    VI. Laws Concerning Worship and Priesthood (Lev 1:1–Num 10:10)
    VII. Wanderings in the Wilderness (Num 10:11–36:13)
    VIII. The Law Reinterpreted (Deut 1–34)

Date, Unity, and Authorship

It remains for us to look briefly at the questions surrounding the date, unity, and authorship of the Pentateuch. There are two major schools of thought regarding these questions. The traditional view has been that Moses himself wrote these books in substantially their present form sometime during Israel's forty years in the wilderness.

The evidence cited in support of this position includes a number of items. First, Moses is said to have written several specific passages found in the Pentateuch (see Exod 17:14; 24:4-8; 34:4-8; Num 33:1-2; Deut 31:9-13, 16-22). Second, other Hebrew Scripture references seem to assume Mosaic authorship of the Pentateuch (see Josh 1:7-8; 8:31; 22:9; 1 Kgs 2:3; 2 Kgs 14:6; 21:8; Ezra 6:18; Neh 13:1). Third, some New Testament passages seem to take for granted that Moses is the author (see Matt 8:4; 19:8; Mark 1:44; 10:4-5; Luke 5:14; 20:37; 24:27, 44; John 5:46-47; 7:19).

The second view calls these assumptions into question. The theory of Mosaic authorship of these books, at least in their present form, began to be questioned about two and a half centuries ago, although occasional doubts were voiced even earlier. Some of the problems were so obvious that even a casual reader might note them. How, for instance, could Moses have written Genesis, since it deals with persons and events belonging to a period more than four hundred years before he was born (see Exod 12:40f.)? If Moses wrote the Pentateuch, why is he consistently referred to in the third person (see Exod 2:11; 3:1; etc.)? How could Moses have written the account of his own death (see Deut 34:1-8)? Who would have taken Moses seriously if he had described himself as "very humble, more so than anyone else on the face of the earth" (Num 12:3)? Why would Moses have referred to the lands lying east of the Jordan as situated "beyond the Jordan," when he was also east of the Jordan (see Num 22:1; Deut 1:1; 3:8)? Why would Moses have referred to a time when kings were ruling in Israel (see Gen 36:31), when Israel had not even settled in its own land, and when the anointing of its first king still lay more than two hundred years in the future?

Other more serious problems are posed by the literary, historical, and theological data found throughout the Pentateuch. Space does not permit these to be discussed at this point. Additional information can be found in the major Bible dictionaries and Hebrew Scripture introductions. Extensive research in this area has given rise to the view that the books of the Pentateuch came from a variety of sources, extending over a long period of time, and representing the early spiritual history and collective memory of the people of God. The sources are thought to have circulated orally before they were committed to writing.

After the sources were written down, they began to be combined into larger units. This process eventually resulted in the Pentateuch as we now know it. The period during which this took place is thought to have lasted approximately six centuries, from roughly 1000 B.C. to around 400 B.C., in other words, from the reign of David until the time of Ezra.

Major Sources

The major sources of the Pentateuch have come to be known as J, E, D, and P, listed in what is judged to be their correct chronological order. Space will allow for only a brief survey of each.

The first of the sources, J, is dated between 950 and 850 B.C., although it is judged to contain some older materials. It receives its name from its consistent designation of the deity as Yahweh, always rendered in English versions of the Bible as "LORD." The author of this source, known simply as the "Yahwist," was a superb storyteller who knew how to use anthropomorphic language with telling effect. This is especially evident in his telling of the story of creation in Genesis 2:4b-25, as well as the story of the tower of Babel in Genesis 11:1-9. The J materials tend to be clustered in Genesis, although some are also found in other parts of the Pentateuch.

The E source receives its name from its use of Elohim, "God," as its designation for the deity. It is thought to have originated in prophetic circles in Northern Israel between 850 and 750 B.C. Nothing in Genesis 1–11 has been assigned to the E source. Instead, its attention is focused on Israel and its first great leaders, notably Abraham, Jacob, Joseph, and Moses. Special emphasis is placed on the prophetic aspect of the call and career of these great leaders (see Gen 20:7; Deut 18:15-19; 34:10-12). E tends to view God as a transcendent being somewhat remote from the human situation. According to E, God is revealed to humans not through personal encounters but by means of angelic visitations, dreams, or visions. E defined the essence of true religion as "the fear of God." Some of the passages where E's criteria may be examined are Genesis 15:1-6, 13-16; 20:1-18; 21:8-21; 22:1-19. Some scholars believe that the J and E materials were combined to form a continuous record sometime in the late pre-exilic period.

The D source is confined to the book of Deuteronomy, and its composition is usually dated in the seventh century B.C. Since it has not been integrated into the other sources, it will be treated in more detail in the section on Deuteronomy. Only a summary of its basic characteristics is needed herre. Deuteronomy takes the form of a series of Mosaic sermons reinterpreting the Torah to Israelites who were one generation removed from the covenant-making ceremony at Sinai. They were gathered on the eastern side of the Jordan waiting to go in and possess the land promised to their ancestors more than four centuries earlier (see Gen 15:7-16; Exod 12:40-41). Deuteronomy was designed to teach them what they must do as the people of God in order to find prosperity, security, and longevity in the land they were about to enter (see Deut 5:33; 11:9; 22:7; 32:47). Because of its strong exhortations to obedience to God, D has been called "the Law preached." Deuteronomy stresses the distinctiveness of Israel's religion and warns against compromising alliances with Canaanites and other foreigners (see Deut 7:1-6; 20:16-18). Purity of worship in Israel is to be safeguarded by limiting the offering of sacrifices to one central sanctuary (see Deut 12:2-7), unlike the earlier practice of allowing the offering of sacrifices wherever the Lord's name was caused to be remembered (see Exod 20:24) by the Lord. The rule was one holy God, one separated people, and one central sanctuary.

The Priestly source, abbreviated as P, was the last to be added to the Pentateuch. It begins with the story of creation in Genesis 1:1–2:4a, and includes other materials in Genesis, Exodus, Leviticus (almost the entire book), and Numbers. Priestly materials are marked by an over-riding interest in legal and cultic matters (matters relating to communal worship). These include the emphasis upon Sabbath observance in the first creation story (Gen 2:1-3); instructions for the design and construction of the tabernacle in the wilderness; proper procedures for offering various kinds of sacrifices; rules for the priesthood; rules for observing special religious festivals such as Passover, Pentecost, Tabernacles, and the Day of Atonement; and kosher food regulations. Various law codes are also embedded in the P source, including the Decalogue (Exod 20:1-17), the Book of the Covenant (Exod 20:22–23:33), and the Holiness Code (Lev 17–26). Priestly materials speak of the deity as Elohim ("God") in all passages prior to Exodus 6:2-3, but use Yahweh ("LORD") and Elohim interchangeably after the Lord's revelation of the divine name to Moses (Exod 6:2-3). Other characteristic features of P include the frequent use of genealogical lists; the systematic organization of Israel's history around three covenants made with Noah (Gen 9:7), with Abraham (Gen 17:6), and with Moses (Lev 26:9); and, finally, a highly repetitious style (see Gen 1:1–2:4a).

Final Formation

The five books of the Pentateuch went through a process of formation not unlike that of the four Gospels at the beginning of the New Testament. Each of the Gospels draws upon other sources, while offering its own distinct perspective on the life and teachings of Jesus. As a result, we are afforded a composite image of Christ that is far richer than would have been possible if there had been only one Gospel.

In a comparable manner, the Pentateuch is made up of four major sources that have been combined into an account of creation, the rise of the nations, and the early spiritual history of Israel. Each of these sources makes its own special contribution to the final shape of the whole.

A major difference between the Pentateuch and the Gospels is that, whereas the Gospels developed side by side in separate books, the Pentateuchal sources were woven together in the same books. Furthermore, it is generally acknowledged that there are discrepancies in the way certain events in the life of Christ are reported in the various Gospels (see Matt 20:29-34; Mark 10:46-52; Luke 18:35-43). Readers seem to have more difficulty, however, in accepting the suggestion that there are discrepancies between the various sources of the Pentateuch, and that these were often allowed to stand side by side without being harmonized.

For example, the order of creation in the P account (Gen 1:1–2:4a) differs widely from that found in the adjoining J account (2:4b-25). Similarly, the P account of the flood reports that Noah took two of every kind of animal, both clean and unclean, with him into the ark to keep them alive (6:19-20; 7:8-9). However, the J account, which has been combined with this account, clearly specifies that Noah was commanded to take seven pairs of all clean animals (in other words, animals fit for sacrifice) with him into the ark (7:2-5). The explanation seems to be that the J writer anticipated the need for extra clean animals so that Noah might offer a sacrifice soon after leaving the ark (see 8:20).

When it is stated that the Pentateuchal sources have been woven together, there is one important exception. Deuteronomy was not combined with the others but has always been allowed to stand apart at the end of the Pentateuch. In this respect it resembles the Gospel of John, which scholars have found difficult to harmonize with the synoptic Gospels (Matthew, Mark, and Luke). The resemblance goes even deeper than this, for both Deuteronomy and John's Gospel are more theological in character than the books with which they are grouped. For instance, each gives a profound interpretation of God's presence with God's people (see Deut 12:5-7; John 1:14).

It seems probable that the priestly writer (or writers) put the finishing touches on the Pentateuch sometime around 400 B.C. In so doing, they hoped to restore the authority of the Law of Moses and to kindle in the Jewish exiles still left in Babylon the hope of a fresh purging from sin and a triumphal return to Jerusalem.

It was evidently this newly completed Pentateuch that Ezra the scribe brought with him from Babylon in 458 B.C. (see Ezra 7:6, 10, 14). Called "the book of the law of Moses," it became an instrument of spiritual renewal when Ezra read it aloud to all the tribes assembled in

Jerusalem (see Neh 8:1ff.). These books then became the canonical core around which the remainder of the Hebrew Scriptures took shape.

The Nature of Biblical Truth

We live in an age that is often confused about the kind of truth presented in the Bible, especially in the early chapters of Genesis. Some suppose they are honoring the Bible when they ascribe to it ultimate authority in such areas as science, archaeology, anthropology, geology, and so on. The same passage that warns against taking away from the words of Scripture also forbids our adding to them (Rev 21:18-19). Truth must be defended not only against its enemies but also against its overzealous friends. History is replete with examples of "super-believers," persons who postulate too much about the Bible. To make claims for the Bible that it does not make for itself, even high-sounding claims, is hardly an appropriate way to honor it.

The truth we encounter in the Bible is stated in terms that are sometimes meant to be taken literally and sometimes figuratively. In both instances the controlling purpose is to teach and not merely to inform. In other words, the aim of Genesis is not merely to give us the facts about creation or the early history of Israel, but also to convince us that the same God who shaped the world and guided Israel's history is our Creator, Savior, and Sovereign, and that this God merits our total obedience. It is truth that presses us for commitment.

Biblical truth, as over against mere mathematical or scientific truth, is often described as "existential" truth, that is, truth about our existence in relation to God, to other persons about us, and to our total environment. Early stories of creation, the garden of Eden, the tree of knowledge, the talking serpent, the flood, and the tower of Babel invite us to ponder truth in parabolic form, truth that differs from and yet does not conflict with scientific truth. Through such stories we gain reliable knowledge about our personal existence before God, our dependence upon God, our proneness to rebel against God, and our need of reconciliation to our Creator.

Every page of the Bible illustrates how persons who wished to express truths about God, even inspired truths, were obliged to do so within the confines of their own language. Prophets and apostles alike confessed that God's ways were not their ways, nor God's thoughts their thoughts (Isa 55:8-9). Even in their most inspired moments, prophets and apostles were only able to see through a glass darkly (1 Cor 13:12). How could it be otherwise when they were trying to describe the indescribable?

One way biblical writers dealt with their task was through the use of metaphors, especially when referring to the personal attributes and activities of God. They described God and God's ways through a variety of images borrowed from their own cultural environment and thus more intelligible to their listeners.

Some of the more familiar metaphors for God are rock (Deut 32:15), shepherd (Ps 23:1), fountain (Jer 17:13), lion (Hos 13:7-8), and eagle (Deut 32:11). To suggest that God is to be identified with any of the above in a literal sense would not be true, but to claim, for example, that God is *like* a shepherd illustrates a technique that good teachers have always used. The symbolic in relation to God are not less true than the literal. Often it is the most effective way to present truths that would otherwise be difficult to understand.

Another group of metaphors found throughout the Bible is related to God as an authority figure. The authority figures that the Israelites encountered most often in their daily lives were parents and rulers. What better way to stress God's dignity and authority over Israel and the nations than through the metaphors of parenthood and kingship? Parenting metaphors included those of fatherhood (see 2 Sam 7:14; Ps 89:26; Jer 31:9; Hos 11:1; Mal 1:6) and also of motherhood (Deut 32:11-12; Ps 131:2; Isa 49:15).

Divine authority on a broader scale has been expressed through metaphors of kingship. Although the Pentateuch seldom makes reference to God as king, this concept is implicit in the whole process of covenant making and lawgiving at Sinai. Because God rules without a rival, God can make decrees and demand that these be strictly observed (Exod 20:1-3; Deut 6:4-5). The call for obedience is expressed in a variety of verbs, including "fear," "honor," "obey," "bow down," and "serve." Earthly kings demanded the respect of their subjects; surely God could do no less.

A final group of metaphors is known as anthropomorphisms, which is simply the ascribing of human characteristics and behavioral patterns to God. It means speaking of God almost as if one were speaking of a human being living and walking upon the earth. Such metaphors are found throughout the Bible, although they are clearly not meant to be taken literally. Otherwise, there would not be so many passages warning us against regarding God as a human being like ourselves (see Num 23:19; 1 Sam 15:29; Job 9:32; Ps 8:4; Hos 11:9). It is emphatically stated that God is spirit and not flesh, unlike the Egyptians and their horses (Isa 31:3). It is impossible to reproduce God's likeness in any image made by human hands (Isa 40:18-26).

On the other hand, it is difficult for ordinary folks such as ourselves to grasp such an exalted and transcendent view of God. It may even make God seem distant and unapproachable. For this reason the Bible begins to speak of God in incarnational language long before the Incarnation itself takes place.

The early chapters of Genesis are filled with anthropomorphical metaphors. For instance, God "forms" the first human being out of the dust of the earth and then "breathes" life into the being's nostrils (2:7). God then "plants" a garden in Eden (2:8). Later God causes a deep sleep to fall upon the human creature, and then God removes a rib and "builds" it into a woman (2:22). God comes "walking" in the garden in the cool part of the day (3:8). The Creator "rests" on the seventh day of creation week (2:2). Later God "sees" the wickedness of human beings and "is sorry" to have created them (6:5-6). After the flood, God "smells" the pleasing odor of Noah's sacrifice and pronounces a blessing upon Noah (8:21).

The presence of these and other anthropomorphisms in the early chapters of Genesis in no way detracts from the glory and majesty of the Creator. All would agree that these are some of the most inspiring chapters of the Bible. The simplicity of their metaphorical language makes it easier for us to grasp what God is like and how we should relate to this One who created us.

For Further Reading

Alter, Robert. *The Art of Biblical Narrative*. New York: Basic Books, 1981.

Childs, Brevard S. *Introduction to the Old Testament as Scriptures*, 112-35. Philadelphia: Fortress Press, 1979.

Clines, David, J. A. *The Theme of the Pentateuch*. JSOT Supplement Series,10. Sheffield England: Department of Biblical Studies, University of Sheffield, 1978.

Friedman, Richard Elliott. "Torah (Pentateuch)." In *Anchor Bible Dictionary*. Vol. 6. New York: Doubleday, 1992.

Gregory, Russell I. "Sources of the Pentateuch," In *Mercer Dictionary of the Bible*. Macon GA: Mercer University Press, 1990.

Jenks, Alan W. "Elohist." In *Anchor Bible Dictionary*. Vol. 2. New York: Doubleday, 1992.

Joines, Karen Randolph. "Yahwist." In *Mercer Dictionary of the Bible*. Macon GA: Mercer University Press, 1990.

Sanders, James A. "Hermeneutics," In *The Interpreter's Dictionary of the Bible*. Supplementary Volume. Nashville: Abingdon, 1976.

_____. *Torah and Canon*. Philadelphia: Fortress Press, 1972.

Whybray, R. Norman. *Introduction to the Pentateuch*, 1-28. Grand Rapids:William B. Eerdmans Publishing Co. 1995.

Chapter 1

Before Abraham Was

Genesis 1–11

Genesis is the book of beginnings. It recounts the beginning of everything—everything, that is, except God. The Creator is simply there, in the beginning. The Bible makes no effort either to define God or to defend God's existence. It merely assumes that God is the uncreated Creator, who existed before creation began, who is not to be identified with creation, and who is in no way dependent upon creation.

The Seven-Day Creation Story

1:1–2:4a

The first account of creation bears a "family likeness" to creation stories originating elsewhere in the ancient world. Such stories circulated among many of Israel's neighbors, including the Sumerians, Akkadians, Babylonians, Hittites, Egyptians, and Assyrians. While similar to the biblical account, these stories are nevertheless inferior to it because they reflect the culture and religious beliefs of the countries that produced them. Polytheistic cultures, for example, always attributed creation to a host of gods, often working in opposition to one another. The Israelites, on the other hand, viewed creation as the unassisted and unopposed work of the one supreme God. There is never the slightest suggestion that other gods even existed, much less posed a threat to God's plan of creation.

Creation Outside Genesis

There are many biblical references to creation outside the book of Genesis. It is a favorite theme in the Prophets, especially in the book of Isaiah (see 40:26, 28; 42:5; 43:1; 44:24; 45:5-7, 12, 18; 48:13). Amos celebrates God as creator in a series of short hymns (see 4:13; 5:8-9; 9:5-6). The book of Job comes to a climax in chapters 38–42, where the theme is the wonder of God's work as creator.

Apart from Genesis, however, there is no other book as rich in its celebration of creation-faith as the book of Psalms. A few psalms make only passing reference to creation (see Ps 24:1-2; 95:3-6; 96:4-5; 100:3; 136:3-9). In others, however, it is the main focus of attention (see Ps 8; 19:1-6; 29; 104; 148). These psalms were written to evoke a response of praise to the Creator from all created beings.

The Earth as Formless and Empty

When God set to work creating the earth, it was "formless and empty" (Gen 1:2 NIV). The Hebrew word for "formless" is *tohu*, a word that normally stands for a barren desert (see Deut 32:10; Job 12:24; Ps 107:40). The companion word for "empty" is *vohu*. It occurs only three times in the Hebrew Scriptures and is always immediately preceded by the word *tohu* (see Gen 1:2; Isa 34:11; Jer 4:23). When used together in this manner, the two words denote a condition of utter chaos. Three problems are symptomatic of the earth's being *tohu*: the darkness, a watery abyss, and an unformed and lifeless earth. These problems are addressed in succession on the first three days of creation. The problem of darkness vanished with the creation of light (Gen 1:3-5). The watery abyss was brought under control by the creation of a firmament arching above the earth and making possible its oceans and its atmosphere (Gen 1:6-8). Finally, on the third day, the dry land appeared, thus completing the three spheres or regions where the remaining acts of creation were to take place. The three spheres were water, air (including atmosphere), and land.

The problem of the emptiness (*vohu*) of these spheres still remained to be addressed. This was done on the fourth, fifth, and sixth days of creation. On the fourth day the firmament was populated with sun, moon, and stars. The fifth day saw the sky filled with birds and the seas stocked with all kinds of marine life. The sixth day brought animals and humans to inhabit the dry land areas of the earth. In its final state, the earth was no longer *tohu* (formless) or *vohu* (empty). It was God's handiwork, filled with all things good and beautiful.

The Days of Creation

Perhaps no part of the creation story has stirred up so much debate as the seven "days" during which the creation took place. Scholars have been unable to agree on whether the days should be interpreted literally or figuratively. Should we accept the view that the creation was completed in a mere 168-hour period (7 x 24)? Or should we take into account the scientific evidence that suggests that the universe is several billion years old? We will look briefly at some of the representative answers that have been proposed for these questions.

(1) Scientific creationists argue that the world was created in six literal twenty-four-hour days, and that creation occurred about 10,000 years ago. Advocates of this position have attempted to reshape scientific theory in order to make it support a literal interpretation of the Bible. What is called "flood geology" is used by them to explain the "seeming" antiquity of earth's geological formations. These persons

still pay lip service to the Bible *and* science, but they have been able to do so only by creating their own revised version of science.

(2) A second proposal is known as the "gap" theory. Proponents of this theory argue that a creation of vast magnitude took place billions of years ago, and is described in Genesis 1:1: "In the beginning God created the heavens and the earth." This first creation was later laid waste by an act of divine judgment, as evidenced by what is taken to be the correct translation of Genesis 1:2: "The earth was a formless void, and darkness came over the face of the deep." Sometime later, according to this theory, God set about recreating the universe, and it is this second creation that is described in the seven-day framework of Genesis 1:3–2:4a. It is believed that there was enough room in the "gap" between the two phases of creation to fit all the geological ages proposed by modern science.

Perhaps the best-known version of the "gap" theory is that presented in the footnotes to Genesis 1 in the Scofield Reference Bible.[1] It suggests that, after the initial creation, the earth underwent "a cataclysmic change as the result of a divine judgment." Scofield holds that this judgment was the result of "a previous testing and fall of angels," of which he finds traces in Ezekiel 28:12-15 and Isaiah 14:9-14. He further states that "the face of the earth bears everywhere the marks of such a catastrophe." This theory represents a determined effort to square Genesis with the modern scientific view of the origin of the universe.

(3) Others have proposed that the seven days of creation week refer not to seven literal twenty-four-hour days, but to seven vast ages of indeterminate length, during the course of which the universe slowly took shape. This was the view supported by my own seminary professor of the Hebrew Scriptures, Dr. Clyde T. Francisco.[2] Those holding this view are also attempting to square Genesis with the modern scientific view of the world.

The problem with all the views presented thus far, in my opinion, is that they are based upon a faulty presupposition. They seem to assume that scientific or empirical truth is the standard by which all other truth, including religious truth, must be tested and judged. They say, for example, that the Bible must meet the criteria devised by scientists, anthropologists, geologists, historians, and so on, or else it becomes unreliable. This means science has been allowed to become the be-all and end-all of epistemology (the study of how knowledge is gained) in the church. We will continue to arrive at false conclusions so long as we search for modern scientific truth in Hebrew Scripture texts that are at least three thousand years old. We must be willing to let the Bible set its own agenda and humble enough to accept its agenda as our own.[3]

Derek Kidner's approach seems to be a step in the right direction.[4] He suggests in his commentary on Genesis that God's work of creation is described as having been compressed into a seven-day week (when in reality it took much longer) in order to simplify its meaning and to give it a form that human minds could more easily grasp. Kidner describes this approach as "a heavy temporal foreshortening that turns ages into days, [thereby] enabling us to construe and not misconstrue a totality too big for us." He concludes that it is "only pedantry that would quarrel with biblical terms that simplify in order to clarify."

Bruce Vawter has observed that the creation story of Genesis "neither affirms nor denies our scientific knowledge of the universe; it [simply] disregards it."[5] The exciting discoveries of science have made vast improvements in the way we live our lives, but they have not diminished God or made God "an unnecessary hypothesis," as some have affirmed. On the contrary, every scientific advance has enlarged our understanding of God's power and majesty. It surely took a great God to create a universe as great as we are now discovering ours to be.

The Excellence of God's Creation

Three attributes of the creation are presented in Genesis 1:1–2:4a. The first is *goodness*, which reflects the goodness of the Creator. The adjective *tov*, or "good," occurs a total of seven times in this account, each time to describe God's own evaluation of the creation (see 1:4, 10, 12, 18, 21, 25, 31).

The designation of creation as good has important implications for theology as well as for ethics. It means that nothing in God's creation is to be regarded as inherently evil, although any created thing may be put to an evil use. A group called the Gnostics tried to persuade early Christians that the material creation was the work of an inferior god, or demiurge, working in direct opposition to the will of the highest God. The goal of gnostic religion was to liberate the spirits of the elect from their prisons of flesh and raise them to the kingdom of light. The Christian answer to such heresy is that our bodies are temples of the Holy Spirit (1 Cor 6:19-20) and worthy sacrifices to be offered upon God's altar (Rom 12:1).

The second attribute of creation is its *orderliness*. The universe is an orderly creation, from its far-flung galaxies to its smallest atoms. Nature may sometimes seem to be chaotic, but the trained eye can see an orderliness permeating the whole. It is through the exercise of reason that nature's orderliness is perceived. We are summoned to use our intellects to probe the orderly structure of the universe. Christians should never oppose the search for truth in any realm of nature, but should welcome the discoveries of every Galileo and Einstein.

The third attribute of God's creation is its *beauty*. The biblical poet expressed it best: God "has made everything beautiful in its time" (Eccl 3:11a RSV). It is this aspect of nature that first catches our attention and is remembered most fondly.

I will always remember the three months that my wife, Vernice, and I spent on the island of Penang off the west coast of Malaysia in the spring of 1986. We were there for a brief teaching assignment in a mission seminary.

The island of Penang is a veritable paradise, bathed on all sides by the jade-green waters of the Indian Ocean. James Michner once described it as "the pearl of the Orient." This was also the time when I was preparing a manuscript on the book of Genesis. It was almost as if I were doing research in the garden of Eden. Our house was located near the southern tip of the island, on the side of a mountain, and facing the sea. The mountain towering behind us was often shaded in clouds and was covered with jungle forests. Flowering trees and shrubs surrounded our house.

A favorite time of day for my wife and me was the early morning. At the first sign of dawn, choirs of exotic birds gathered in the trees and serenaded us. Monkeys also came early to rob our mango tree of any fruit that might have ripened during the night. Eagles could often be seen circling overhead, gracefully riding the air currents that swept up the face of the mountain. As we watched the sun rising each morning, we were reminded of the words of praise to the Creator in Psalm 104:24: "O Lord, how manifold are thy works! In wisdom hast thou made them all; the earth is full of thy creatures" (KJV).

The Second Creation Account
2:4b-25

Chapters 2:4b–3:24 form a literary unit. Both come from the pen of the J writer. They have their setting in the garden of Eden and describe what took place from the time Adam and Eve became its caretakers until they were expelled because of their disobedience. This section has a fair beginning but a foul ending.

Differences Between the Creation Accounts

The differences between the P account of creation in Genesis 1:1–2:4a and the account in 2:4b-25 are easy to discover.

(1) Their choice of *divine names* is different. The first account (P) uses only *Elohim* ("God"), and it occurs thirty-five times. The later account (J) uses the compound *Yahweh Elohim* ("LORD God"). It appears twenty times in Genesis 2 and 3, but only one other time throughout the rest of the Pentateuch (Exod 9:30).

(2) The *manner in which God creates* is described differently in these two accounts. The first account pictures God as exalted above the earth and somewhat removed from the human scene. Because God is so great in power, God is able to create by a simple word of command (Gen 1:3, 6, 9, 14-15, 24; see Ps 33:6-9). The second account describes creation as a "hands-on" operation. The LORD God "formed" man from dust and then "breathed" life into his nostrils (2:7). The Lord God "planted" a garden and installed the man as its caretaker (2:7-8, 15). Later the Lord God removed a "rib" from the man and made it into a woman (2:21-22).

(3) The two accounts differ in their *description of the state of the world* before God set about to reshape it. The first depicts it as a watery chaos (1:2); the second sees it as a dry, barren desert (2:4b-6).

(4) The *order* in which creation took place also differs. The first account gives a panoramic view of the creation of light, the firmament, dry land and plants, sun, moon and stars, sea creatures and birds, and land animals and humans. The second account describes only the earth and the acts of creation that took place upon it. This earthly phase of creation is described as having taken place in four steps: the creation of man, the planting of a well-watered garden of trees; the creation of animals and birds; and the creation of a woman.

(5) The *creation of human beings* is stated differently in the two accounts. First, the distinction of the sexes is explained in a different way. The first account seems to imply that males and females were created simultaneously (1:27). The second describes the creation of the man and the woman as separate actions (2:7, 21-22). Second, the first account states that humans were created in the image and likeness of God and given dominion over the other forms of life that were upon the earth (1:26-27). The second account pictures the LORD God fashioning a human being (Hebrew: *adam*) from the dust of the ground (*adamah*), much as a potter might shape a vessel (2:7). Later, the woman is created from a part that was removed from *adam* (2:21-22).

(6) The *time frame* is a crucial element in the first account, but it is not even mentioned in the second. The second account makes no mention of the six days during which God worked nor of the seventh day on which God rested. The second account gives no indication as to how long it might have taken the LORD God to make all these things.

(7) The *climax of creation* is stated differently in the two accounts. The first account reaches its climax with the setting aside of the seventh day as a day of sacred rest, a day to be kept holy unto God (Gen 2:2-3; Exod 20:8-11). This was God's way of stating why human beings were created upon the earth. They were created to be involved in a rhythmic cycle of purposeful work and worshipful rest. God blessed the Sabbath and endowed it with recreative power (2:3), just as earlier a special blessing had been given to living creatures (1:22) and human beings (1:28), enabling both to transmit life and vitality to future generations.

The second creation account comes to a climax when the LORD God makes possible the world's first recorded marriage ceremony (2:22-23). The *adam* had been created for companionship, and that need could not be satisfied in the company of animals and birds (2:18-20). It could only be met in union with one who was part of his own flesh and without whom he would always be incomplete and unfulfilled.

This new story of creation in the garden of Eden thus had a wonderful beginning. It's the kind of story we might like to have provided with a different ending, something more like that of a modern fairy tale, "And they lived happily ever after." We know, of course, that real life so often does not turn out that way.

Do the differences between the two Genesis accounts of creation mean that they contradict each other? By no means! They simply were written with different purposes in mind, and each complements the other. We need both to give us a balanced view of God, a Being far above us and yet so very near to us (see Isa 57:15). We also need to explain the paradoxical nature of human beings, created small and yet potentially great (see Ps 8:3-8), formed of dust (Gen 2:7) and yet created in the image of God (Gen 1:27-28). We can be grateful that God has given us these separate stories, for together they help us better to understand who God is as well as who we are.

Paradise Lost

3:1-24

When humans were placed upon the earth, it was so that they might be servants of God but masters of all else. They were granted permission to eat freely of the trees of the garden of Eden, with one notable exception. They were forbidden to eat of the fruit of the tree of knowledge of good and evil, under the penalty of death (2:16-17). They needed to learn that even in Eden there was no such thing as absolute freedom. There can be no meaningful human existence where the boundaries of human freedom are not recognized and respected.

Adam and Eve were spoiled by prosperity. They had been given a paradise, power, authority, and responsibility for their immediate environment. All that they had been given was not enough. They wanted ultimate power, the power to be like God. They were not willing to accept their creatureliness, the limitations of what it meant to be mortal. And then as now, self-deification resulted in alienation from God, family members, neighbors, and even the surrounding flora and fauna of the natural world.

The only person who did not grasp at equality with God was Jesus (Phil 2:5-8). He alone attained to perfect personhood. All other humans have failed. Jesus never rejected the human aspects of the incarnation but always made his will subservient to that of his heavenly Father (Matt 26:39). Jesus' perfect obedience teaches us what it means to be truly human.

The Role of the Serpent

The world has always been fascinated by serpents. Some people have regarded them as symbols of healing (see Num 21:6-9; Mark 6:17-18). Also, serpents have acquired a reputation for wisdom and craftiness (see Gen 3:1-3; Matt 10:16). Because they periodically shed their skins and grow new ones, ancient people concluded that serpents possessed immortality and were like the gods.

The story of the serpent in the garden of Eden has parallels to a similar story in Mesopotamian literature. The *Epic of Gilgamesh* tells of an ancient hero who set out in search of immortality.[6] After a long and dangerous journey, he was given a plant that would impart immortality to those who ate its fruit. On his way home, however, he stopped to bathe in a wayside pool, only to have a serpent come out of the water and eat his plant. He sadly concluded that immortality was for the gods alone.

When we come to the story of the serpent in Genesis, we face the danger that we will read too much into it. The Hebrew Scriptures avoid interpreting the serpent as anything other than one of the animals that God created and placed in the garden of Eden. Adam was supposed to have dominion over it, but, in the end, he let it have dominion over him. The serpent was able to talk, a gift also displayed by Balaam's ass (Num 22:21-30). The earliest recorded identification of the tempter in the garden of Eden with the devil occurs in *The Wisdom of Solomon*, an apocryphal work usually assigned to the latter part of the first century B.C.

The Sequel to Sin

The outcome of the sin of Adam and Eve was not what they had antic-ipated. The serpent had assured them that their eyes would be opened and that they would be like God, knowing good and evil (3:5). Their eyes were opened, but what they actually discovered was not that they were like God, but that they were naked (3:7). And against the biblical background, nakedness is a symbol of weakness, helplessness, vulner-ability, and poverty (see Deut 28:48; Job 1:21; Isa 58:7; Rom 8:35; Rev 3:17).

Partners in Sin

The Bible pictures Adam and Eve as equally guilty before God. They were partners in crime and partners in punishment. Sin is equally serious whether it is committed by someone who is overcome by temptation or by someone who is merely following the crowd. Eve yielded to temptation after an all-out assault by the serpent. Adam followed her example and yielded to temptation without any apparent show of resistance. Perhaps this was why Paul wrote that it was through *man* (italics mine) that sin entered the world (Rom 5:12). Events in the garden of Eden do not offer any grounds whatsoever for male pride or for chauvinism.

A Bitter Harvest

Prior to the disobedience of Adam and Eve there had been peace and harmony in the garden of Eden. But their disobedience transformed the garden into a place of alienation and disharmony. The peaceful days of the past gave way to strife and contention (3:14-19).

First, there was alienation from God. Note, however, that God did not hide from them; on the contrary, it was they who hid from God (3:8). When God inquired about what they had done, both of them offered alibis instead of honest confessions. Their whole demeanor was one of distrust toward God.

Second, they were alienated from each other. When Adam was questioned about his role in these tragic events, he pointed an accusing finger at Eve, and ultimately at God, when he said, "The woman whom *thou* (italics mine) gavest to be with me, she gave me of the tree, and I did eat" (3:12 KJV). How quickly Adam had been stripped of his love and his nobler instincts! His accusation against Eve was a complete reversal of his outburst of joy and delight at first seeing her (3:23-24).

Eve's attitude toward Adam was also changed. Now her love for him was ruled by desire, and physical desire has always been a poor substitute for love (3:16). For the first time in their lives their nakedness made them ashamed and embarrassed to be around each other (3:7-10). They had lost their innocence.

Third, there was alienation between humans and animals, as symbolized by the enmity placed between the offspring of the woman and the offspring of the serpent (3:15). The J writer understood, at least in part, that the ferocity of wild beasts and venomous serpents was in some way related to the burden of human sin. The Bible foretells a time when animals and humans will be reconciled to each other and their lost unity will be restored (Isa 11:6-9; 65:25; Rom 8:21-22).

Fourth, there was alienation between humans and the soil that nourished them. Cultivating the soil and harvesting its produce would no longer be a labor of love, but an endless cycle of toil and tears (3:17-19). In the end, the human body would return to the earth from which it had been taken.

Where Sin Abounded

The curtain falls on the first couple standing outside an Eden to which they could not return. We all know the experience. Some deliberate sin or some stupid mistake destroys our finest opportunity, and no amount of remorse can bring it back.

But all hope is not lost! If Genesis teaches anything about God, it is that God is the God of the second chance. God judged the sin of Adam and Eve, but judgment was tempered with mercy. Before God cast them out of Eden, God provided clothing for the wintry world outside (3:21). And God posted cherubim to guard the way to the tree of life (3:24). We now know that beyond the first Adam there was a Second Adam, one who restored access to the tree of life and opened for us the gates of Paradise (1 Cor 15:45; Rev 22:1-5). "Where sin increased, grace abounded all the more" (Rom 5:20).

From Adam to Noah
4:1–5:32

Two contrasting themes are developed in Genesis 4–11: the growing power of sin and the hidden growth of God's grace. The first indication of sin's growing power was Cain's murder of his brother Abel (4:1-16). When Adam and Eve sinned, they lost fellowship with God; when Cain sinned, he lost touch with both God and his brother. These two accounts epitomize the disruptive power of evil.

For Cain to take the life of another human being was to usurp authority that belonged to God alone (see Gen 9:5-6). In a sense he was imitating the sin of his parents; he was making himself "like God." There are several parallels between the sin stories in Genesis 3 and 4. In each case God confronts the offenders and holds them accountable for what they have done (3:9-11; 4:9-10). In both instances the land loses its productivity because of the sins committed (3:17-19; 4:11-12a). In both stories the offenders are driven from the land where they have been living (3:22-24; 4:12b-14,16). Finally, God provides clothing for Adam and Eve (3:21) and a special mark of protection for Cain (4:15).

Cain's murder of Abel was a senseless act of violence. Abel seems to have always been overshadowed by his older brother. It was customary in Near Eastern society for the firstborn son to occupy the place of privilege in the family. God apparently ignored custom by accepting the sacrifice of Abel and rejecting that of Cain (4:1-5). The latter action so incensed Cain that he invited his brother to go with him to an isolated place with the obvious intention of killing him (4:8). Did Cain think that God would bestow love on him alone, once his brother was out of the picture?

We need to be aware of the sin of Cain! It is so easy for us to resent the grace that God bestows on others, particularly those we regard as inferior to us. It is difficult for us to comprehend that God loves all people without showing favoritism toward any. God refuses to be the enemy of our enemies.

Chapters 4 and 5 contain two significant genealogies, that of Cain (4:17-24) and that of Seth, Adam and Eve's third son (4:25–5:32). The names in both lists are similar (Cain/Kenan; Enoch/Enoch; Irad/Jared; Mehujael/Mahalalel; Methushael/Methuselah; and Lamech/Lamech), although the order in which they stand is somewhat different. The genealogy of Cain begins with one murderer and ends with another, the last being the violent Lamech who boasts of his vengeful reign of terror (14:19-24). This bit of family history helps to explain the moral and spiritual corruption that later prompted God to send the flood.

Adam and Eve's third son, Seth, was seen as the replacement for the ill-fated Abel (4:25). The most significant event of the antediluvian period was when people began to call on the name of the LORD. We are told that this took place in the days of Seth and his descendants (4:26).

The genealogies of the Bible show how history tended to be represented in terms of periods. The genealogy of Seth (4:25–5:32) covers the ten generations from creation to the flood, in other words, from Adam and Eve to Noah. Life spans during this period varied greatly, ranging from 969 years for Methuselah to 365 years for Enoch. The average life span for the period was 857. These ages seem conservative when compared to those of the eight Sumerian kings who are said to have reigned between creation and the flood in the Sumerian account. The reigns of the Sumerian kings are said to have lasted from 43,200 years to a mere 18,600, the grand total for the eight being 241,200 years. Incidentally, the age reported in the Bible for Methuselah implies that he died in the year of the flood.

By placing the genealogy of Cain immediately before that of Seth, the biblical writer points out the two ways in which we may choose to live. The way of Cain is the way of self-centeredness, jealousy, suspicion, and hatred. The way of Seth, in contrast, is the way of prayerful living, service to others, and submission to the will of God. Only the latter way leads to fullness of life.

The Flood and Noah's Ark (6:1–9:7)

The flood story was not written for the entertainment of children in Sunday School. It is a serious part of the unfolding drama of crime, punishment, and redemption contained in the first eleven chapters of Genesis.

We may note four themes that are developed in this story. (1) Sin is cosmic in its origin and in its effect. (2) God hates and punishes sin. (3) God does not hold the righteous responsible for the sins of the unrighteous. When God sent the flood, provision had been made for the sparing of the righteous Noah and his family. (4) The judgment of the flood did not free the world from the threat of wickedness. God applied other solutions to the sin problem until it was time for the ultimate solution, the offering of God's own Son as a sacrifice for sin. It is no accident that early Christians decorated the walls of the catacombs with crude drawings of the box-like ark, which they saw as a foreshadowing of the church of our Lord Jesus Christ.

The Prologue to the Flood (6:1-8)

The brief prologue to the flood tells how the murderous conduct of Cain and his descendants was augmented by the lustful behavior of angels from the heavenly realm (6:1-4). The resulting corruption grieved God and made God regret that humankind had been created (6:5-6). The ensuing flood would have destroyed life on the earth, had it not been for righteous Noah (6:7-8).

The material in 6:1-8 is some of the most obscure in the Bible. A popular view is that "sons of God" is a designation for the good people of the earth, symbolized by the descendants of Seth, while "daughters of humans" refers to the evil people of the earth, symbolized by the descendants of Cain.

Apart from its sexist overtone (Why should women represent the evil in society while men represent the good?), this interpretation ignores the fact that elsewhere in the Hebrew Scriptures the phrase "sons of God" designates heavenly beings or angels (see Job 1:6; 2:1; 38:7; Ps 29:1; 89:6). The heavenly realm is reflected in a number of Hebrew Scripture passages, including Genesis 28:10-17; 1 Kings 22:19-23; and Isaiah 6:1-8.

The most natural meaning of Genesis 6:1-8, therefore, is that it describes an outbreak of rebellion against God in the heavenly court itself. It involved intermarriage between heavenly beings (males) and human beings (females) and thus represented an attempt to unite two realms of existence that God intended should remain apart. The mixing of the human and the divine, the earthly and the heavenly, was strictly forbidden from the beginning. At the same time, however, we should avoid unfounded speculation about the "fall of angels," as is found, for example, in noncanonical sources such as 1 Enoch (6:1-2; 7:2).

The speech in 6:3 has been called "a divine soliloquy." It portrays what Whybray described as "nervousness about the possibility that [human]kind may now go further and seize the immortality which properly belongs only to God."[7]

Immortality is denied to the offspring of the union between the sons of God and the daughters of men, and their maximum lifetime is fixed at 120 years (6:3). The children born to these marriages are called Nephilim (6:4), meaning "fallen ones" (fallen from their heavenly status), and are described as a race of giants. Elsewhere in the Hebrew Scriptures they are called Rephaim (see Num 13:32-33; Deut 2:10-11, 20-21; 3:11; Josh 12:4; 17:15).

Babylonian Parallels to the Flood Story

There are ancient Babylonian parallels to the story of the flood and the lifesaving ark. One is found in tablet XI of the *Gilgamesh Epic*. A longer account bears the name of the hero *Atrahasis*.[8] It tells how the Babylonian high gods created humans from clay mixed with the blood and spirit of a slain rebel god. Humans were then appointed to do menial tasks for the gods, such as providing them with the food of their sacrifices. Humans began to multiply at such a pace, however, that their noise level made it difficult for the gods to sleep. The gods therefore decided to wipe out the human race with a flood, but this plot was thwarted by a friendly god, Enki, who secretly advised

Atrahasis how to escape. Atrahasis built an ark for his family and the animals, and through him the human race was reestablished after the flood, much to the displeasure of the council of gods.

Genesis has taken the polytheistic elements out of these ancient flood stories. It cites humankind's moral turpitude and not mere noise as the cause behind the flood. The flood is sent by God alone and not by a council of gods. The decision to spare the righteous Noah is taken freely and spontaneously. The blessings pronounced after the flood (9:1-3) are an unqualified reaffirmation of the blessings given at creation (1:27-29). The only change involved permission for people to kill animals for food, and this was given because of human necessity and not because of divine displeasure. The Babylonian stories illustrate the profound differences between Israel's God and the gods of paganism.

God's Commitment to Creation (8:20-22)

Noah's first act upon leaving the ark was to erect an altar and offer a burnt offering to the Lord. Praise was the only appropriate response to the deliverance he had experienced. God's reaction involved a fresh pledge of commitment to the creation. This was done in spite of the fact that there had been no improvement in human nature as a result of the flood. Actually, the story closes with a rather pessimistic assessment of the whole human situation. The initial reason God sent the flood was that "the wickedness of humankind was great in the earth, and every inclination of the thoughts of their hearts was only evil continually" (6:5). We might have expected the flood to correct this situation, but such was not the case. When God pledged never again to judge the earth with a flood, that decision was grounded not in humankind's penitent spirit but in the impenetrable hardness of the human heart. God said, "I will never again curse the ground because of humankind, *for the inclination of the human heart is evil from youth*" (8:21b, italics mine).

This seemingly illogical statement led Brueggeman to observe, "The flood has effected no change in humankind. But it has effected an irreversible change in God, who now will approach . . . creation with an unlimited patience and forbearance."9

God's Covenant with Noah (9:1-17)

God sealed the commitment to Noah and all humankind after Noah with a covenant (9:8-11). It was in the form of a treaty made, not between equals, but between a sovereign leader and subjects. It was unilateral, which means it was undertaken at God's initiative and without any preliminary conditions being imposed on the beneficiaries. In brief, it was a covenant of grace.

This is the first covenant mentioned in the Bible. It has much in common with the Abrahamic covenant in Genesis 17. Each is said to have been "established" between God and God's servants (9:11; 17:7). Each is called an "everlasting covenant" (9:16; 17:13, 19). Each is sealed with a sign, the first with a rainbow (9:12-17) and the second with the sign of circumcision (17:11).

The rainbow projected on the face of the storm cloud is a powerful symbol of hope born out of trouble. Since the Hebrew word for "rainbow" is the same as that used for "war bow," it meant that God had ended hostilities against the world and had hung up a war bow on the clouds in full view of all who had survived the flood. Never again, regardless of the depth of human depravity, would God destroy the earth with a flood. God would never forget to be merciful (9:16).

Noah's Sons and Their Descendants (9:18–11:30)

The closing part of the primeval history treats of the last days of Noah, the exploits of his sons, and the listing of their descendants down to Abraham. It also tells of the defiant building of a city and a tower, resulting in the worldwide dispersal of the builders and the confusion of their language.

Noah's Drunkenness (9:18-28)

The story of Noah's vineyard and subsequent drunkenness was not written to censure him for drinking too much, since he was probably ignorant of the intoxicating effects of wine. It was written to highlight the sin of Ham and to explain the curse placed upon his son Canaan. This story rounds out the record of family conflict and strife in the primeval period, a record that included marital conflict (Adam and Eve), sibling rivalry and fratricide (Cain and Abel), and conflict between father and son (Noah and Ham/Canaan).

The account of Noah's drunkenness seems to be deliberately obscure, with important details having been left out. Why, for example, is Ham referred to as Noah's youngest son, when elsewhere he is listed as the middle son (5:32; 6:10; 7:13; 9:18; 10:1)? What does it mean that Ham "saw his father's nakedness" (9:22)? Was this simply a show of disrespect for his naked father, or does this imply some act of sexual perversion against his father? The latter position seems to have been popular among ancient Jewish rabbis. Some argued that Ham castrated his father, while others described Ham's sin as that of sodomy.

The most baffling question of all is why Ham's sin caused his son Canaan to be cursed. Was this simply a case of the father's sin being visited upon the son (see. Exod 20:5)? Or was the son also involved in the father's sin? In any event, the sin of Ham resulted in Canaan's being condemned to become "a slave of slaves" (9:25), meaning "the lowest of slaves," to the more favored brothers, Shem and Japheth (9:26-27). This seems to mean that God permitted the Israelites, the descendants of Shem, and the Philistines, the descendants of Japheth, to mount a two-pronged attack on the Canaanites around 1200 B.C., paving the way for the conquest of Canaan. The Canaanites were notorious for their depravity (see Lev 18:3-4, 24-28; 20:22-23), and the Israelites believed they had a moral right to seize their land (see Exod 33:2; Deut 9:4; Josh 3:10). The biblical view is that a nation's fate is inevitably bound up with the character of its people (Prov 14:34).

The Table of the Nations (chap. 10)

Genesis 10 furnishes a picture of unity in the midst of diversity. Earlier genealogies in Genesis 4 and 5 are made up of the names of individuals, but this one constitutes a roll call of the nations, with brief reference to some of their more outstanding leaders (see 10:8-9). Its international character is indicated by the recurring refrain: "These are the descendants of . . . by their families, their languages, their lands, and their nations" (vv. 5, 20, 31, 32). The total number of nations found here is seventy, a number symbolic of completion. The theological assumption underlying this chapter is that God's sovereignty extends to all nations, that God provides for all, and that all are accountable to their Creator.

The additional statement in verse 32 that these were the nations that spread abroad after the flood points backward to the command given to Noah and his sons to multiply and fill up the earth (9:1). It also anticipates the scattering of the nations that followed the building of a city and the tower of Babel (11:1-9). Chapter 10 lists the scattered nations; chapter 11 explains why they were scattered.

The Scattering of the Nations (11:1-9)

Genesis 11:1-9 describes civilization at its highest point in the prepatriarchal period. Its description of urban expansion and advanced building technology makes it sound almost modern. Today's city architects would be rewarded for such innovative planning. Was it childish of God to want to prevent these people from demonstrating what they were capable of doing on their own (see 11:6)?

What the people were doing was clearly subversive. Their desire was to sever all dependence on God. They wanted to build a city on earth, but to link it to heaven by means of their "skyscraper" tower. They thought this would give them ready access to the realm of the divine. Theirs was the sin of Adam and Eve all over again, except on a grander scale. They had to learn the hard way that rebellion against God only gives one the illusion of independence.

They were also motivated by fear, the fear that they would be scattered abroad over the face of the earth (11:4). The Hebrew verb "to scatter" is often used in a negative sense, meaning to suffer defeat or to be forcibly removed from one's land (see Num 10:35; 1 Sam 1:11; 1 Kgs 22:17; Neh 1:8; Ezek 36:19). Ironically, what they were trying to prevent was precisely what happened. The end result was dispersal among the nations and the inability to communicate with one another (11:9). Their unfinished city became a monument to their arrogant pride and ambition (11:8).

God's New Way (11:10-30)

In chapter 11, the genealogy of Shem is traced through ten generations, matching the ten generations of Seth in chapter 5. These two genealogies are also alike in that each culminates in an individual who offers hope for the future, first Noah (5:32), and then Abraham (11:26). Each represented God's new way.

Before the tower of Babel experience, God's judgment had always been tempered with mercy. God provided clothing for Adam and Eve; a protective mark for Cain; and an ark for Noah, his family, and animals. However, in the account of the scattering that followed the building of the tower of Babel there is no mention of mercy. But it is precisely here that the genealogy of Shem becomes so important. It brings us down to Abram and Sarai (10:29), during whose lifetime the scattering of the nations probably took place. Hope for the future centered in these two. Through them and their descendants God expected to establish a new beachhead in human history and to eventually reclaim the nations as God's own (see Phil 2:9-10; Rev 11:15).

At the time Shem's genealogy was prepared, however, the hope embodied in Abram and Sarai remained obscure. We read in 11:30 that "Sarai was barren; she had no child." To overcome Sarai's sterility and to transform the curse of the nations into a blessing could be accomplished by nothing less than a miracle from above. God, who had first called a world into existence out of nothingness, must now call a nation into being out of barrenness. The latter plan caused Brueggemann to treat Genesis 1–11 under the heading, "The Sovereign

Call of God." It would have been entirely appropriate if the primeval history had ended with the words, "to be continued."

Notes

[1]*The Holy Bible*, ed. C. I. Scofield, New and Improved Edition (New York: Oxford University Press, 1917) 3-6.

[2]Clyde T. Francisco, "Genesis," in *The Broadman Bible Commentary* (Nashville: Broadman Press, 1973) 1:120, 123.

[3]For a fuller discussion along these lines, see Clark H. Pinnock, "Climbing Out of a Swamp: The Evangelical Struggle to Understand the Creation Texts," *Interpretation* 43 (1989): 143-15.

[4]Derek Kidner, "Genesis," in *Tyndale Old Testament Commentaries* (London: Tyndale Press, 1967) 54-58.

[5]Bruce Vawter, *A Path Through Genesis* (New York: Sheed and Ward, 1956) 49.

[6]"Epic of Gilgamesh," Tablet XI, lines 277-89, 2nd ed. *Ancient Near Eastern Texts*, ed. James B. Pritchard (Princeton: Princeton University Press, 1955) 96.

[7]R. N. Whybray, *Introduction to the Pentateuch* (Grand Rapids: Eerdmans Publishing Co., 1995) 33.

[8]W. G. Lambert and Alan R. Millard, *Atrahasis: The Babylonian Story of the Flood* (Oxford: Oxford University Press, 1969).

[9]Walter Brueggemann, *Genesis* (Atlanta: John Knox Press, 1982) 81.

For Further Reading

Brueggemann, Walter. *Genesis*, 11-104. Atlanta: John Knox Press, 1982.

Mann, Thomas W. *The Book of the Torah*, 10-29. Atlanta: John Knox Press, 1988.

Sarna, Nahum M. "Genesis." In *The J.P.S. Torah Commentary*, 3-87. Philadelphia: The Jewish Publication Society, 1989.

Vawter, Bruce. *A Path Through Genesis*, 31-110. New York: Ward and Sheed, 1956.

Weaver, John D. *In the Beginning God: Modern Science and the Christian Doctrine of Creation*. Oxford: Regent's Park College; Macon GA: Smyth & Helwys, 1994.

Young, Davis A. *The Biblical Flood*. Grand Rapids: William B. Eerdmans Publishing Co., 1995.

Chapter 2

Pilgrims of Faith

Genesis 11:27–25:11

In September 1952, Vernice and I were aboard a ship bound for Brazil, where we had been appointed to serve as missionaries. Our voyage lasted two weeks and involved only one stop between New Orleans and Rio de Janeiro. It was a refueling stop at the port of St. Thomas in the Virgin Islands.

On the afternoon of our arrival at St. Thomas, we gathered with other passengers on the main deck of the ship. We noted that the entrance to the harbor was very narrow and flanked on either side by partially submerged reefs. However, the ship's pilot guided us safely through the narrow channel and into the harbor.

We were allowed a brief shore leave with instructions to be back on board shortly before midnight to resume our voyage. When midnight came and the ship was leaving the harbor, some of us wondered out loud how the pilot would be able to navigate the ship in the dark. A crewman overheard us and pointed to something we had not noticed. On a sloping hill above the harbor three series of beacons had been lighted. They were arranged somewhat like the approach lights to a large airport. We watched as the pilot maneuvered the ship into such a position that the beacons formed a straight path directly behind us. This put us on course and enabled us to pass safely from the harbor and out into the broad ocean beyond.

This experience stuck in my memory. Across the intervening years, it has served as an illustration of what it means to journey by faith. Often the way before us is dark and the future unpredictable. Unable to chart our course with confidence, we become afraid, and all too often our fears immobilize us. What we need is a guiding star, a point of reference that is steadfast and sure. And this can be found only in God. We need to look to God to find guidance for our lives. When our wills are brought into line with God's will, the road becomes clear, and we can move ahead without fear or hesitation. It was this assurance that led the psalmist to say to God, "Even the darkness is not dark to you; the night is as bright as the day, for darkness is as light to you" (Ps 139:12).

The World of the Patriarchs

There is nothing new about setting out on a pilgrimage of faith. Our study of Genesis 12–50 will introduce us to a variety of men and women who undertook such a pilgrimage. "Patriarch" is the title given to the men in this group, but their wives also deserve recognition alongside them. The three principal patriarchs were Abraham, Isaac, and Jacob (see Exod 3:6; 6:3; Deut 1:8; 1 Kgs 18:36). The followers of three world religions—Judaism, Christianity, and Islam—all claim these three as their spiritual forefathers. Joseph and Judah also deserve to be included among the patriarchs whose work is highlighted in Genesis.

Date

Though the patriarchs cannot be dated with precision, a comparison of archaeological and biblical data places them somewhere in the period between 2000 and 1500 B.C. Scholars connect Abraham's migration to Canaan with other large-scale people movements going on at the same time. The Amorites, for example, were pouring into northern Mesopotamia and establishing city-states as far south as Canaan (see Gen 15:21). Ezekiel 16:3 preserves a tradition that the Israelites themselves were descendants of the Amorites and of a related group called the Hittites.

It was once thought that the patriarchs came upon the world scene at the very threshold of human history and wandered about in a world that was largely uninhabited. Archaeology has shown this to be a mistaken idea. Abraham's native city of Ur was founded around 3700 B.C., and, assuming that he was called to leave Ur around 2000 B.C., it was already a very ancient city. When Abraham later migrated to Canaan, he found it to be a thickly populated area filled with walled cities over which competing powers had already been fighting for a thousand years or more. When famine caused Abraham and Sarah to flee to Egypt, they entered a land whose pyramids had already been standing at least five hundred years. In a real sense, therefore, the patriarchs were relative latecomers on the stage of world history.

Aramean Connections

The predominant tradition concerning the racial origin of the patriarchs is that they belonged to a Semitic group called Arameans. This tradition was preserved in a creed that later Israelites recited as they offered firstfruits at the altar: "A wandering Aramean was my ancestor" (Deut 26:5). Abraham sent a servant to find a wife for Isaac from among the patriarch's kinsfolk in *Aram-naharaim* (Gen 24:10), translated "Mesopotamia" in the RSV, but whose literal meaning is "Aram of the two rivers." The rivers in question were the Tigris and the Euphrates.

According to Genesis 11:31, Abraham's father migrated from Ur to Haran, an Aramean city located in the northwestern part of Mesopotamia near Carchemish. The region is known in the Hebrew Scriptures as Paddan-aram. Isaac's wife Rebekah was "the daughter of Bethuel the Aramean of Paddan-aram" (25:20). Furthermore, it was to Haran in Paddan-aram that Jacob also journeyed in search of a wife (28:5, 10). Why Terah, the father of Abraham, stopped in Haran instead of completing the journey to Canaan is not made clear. He was still among his own relatives in Haran, and perhaps he was not yet ready to cut the ties that bound him to them. It remained for Abraham to complete the journey to Canaan without his father.

Both Ur and Haran were important centers for the worship of the moon god Sin. In fact, names such as Terah, Sarah, Milcah, and Laban —names common to Abraham's family—all reflect a background of moon worship. The pagan origins of Abraham's ancestors were still remembered and acknowledged many centuries later. Joshua reminded the Israelites of this in his address at Shechem: "Long ago your ancestors—Terah and his sons Abraham and Nehor—lived beyond the Euphrates and served other gods" (Josh 24:2). It is marvelous that God was able to form a new nation out of such a pagan beginning.

The patriarchs also inherited a legal code from their Amorite and Aramean ancestors. Clay tablets from the excavation of Nuzi, an ancient city in Northwestern Mesopotamia, have been especially helpful in this regard.[1] For example, according to Nuzi law, a man who had no male heir could make his son-in-law his heir. If a son was born later, however, the son-in-law would lose his inheritance rights. This law helps to explain what happened to Jacob as a member of Laban's household. When Jacob arrived in Haran, Laban, having no sons of his own, apparently adopted Jacob through Jacob's marriage to Rachel and Leah. The account in Genesis suggests that sons were later born to Laban and that this complicated matters for Jacob and convinced him that he should return to Canaan.

Nuzi law also permitted a childless couple to adopt a son to care for them in their old age. Upon their death he would inherit their property. However, if a son was later born to the couple, the adopted son would lose all claim to their property. This law sheds light on events described in Genesis 15:1-6. Abraham was apparently planning to adopt his servant Eliezer as his heir because of Sarah's continued barrenness.

Another Nuzi law permitted a barren wife to give her handmaid to her husband to serve as a surrogate wife and to bear him an heir. This explains Sarah's gift of Hagar to Abraham (16:1-4) and Rachel's later gift of Bilhah to Jacob (30:1-8). Nuzi law also forbade the mistreatment or expulsion of the surrogate wife, even if the original wife later bore children of her own. This probably accounts for Abraham's reluctance to drive out Hagar and Ishmael following the birth of Isaac (21:8-11).

Religion

It is well to introduce the subject of the religion of the patriarchs by looking briefly at the religion of the Canaanites.[2] Canaanite religion has been much better understood since the discovery from 1929 onward of a major treasure of clay tablets called the Ras Shamra texts. These texts were found at ancient Ugarit near the Mediterranean coast in northern Syria.[3]

The Canaanite gods included El, his consort Asherah, and their son Baal Hadad. The latter is referred to in the Hebrew Scriptures simply as Baal. His consort was Anath. Baal was the giver of rain and thus the sustainer of vegetation. His greatest enemy was Mot (Death), who annually destroyed him and from whose power Anath had to rescue him, making possible the return of the life-giving rains.

The worship of Baal was designed to maintain the processes of nature in harmonious balance and to promote fertility in the fields, among the flocks, and in the females of each tribe. One way this was done was through the choice of certain women to be "holy" and set apart as sacred prostitutes at the Baal shrines. To do this was to place the fertility of women and symbolically of fields and flocks under the maintenance and protection of Baal.

Patriarchal religion had an ethical and moral dimension that was missing in Baalism. The practice of religious prostitution, whether by men or women, was strictly forbidden in Israel (Deut 23:17-18). Such behavior was looked upon as "an abomination," in other words, as something grossly out of harmony with the revelation of God's will and character. When the Israelites ignored this, as they did at Baal-peor, their punishment became an object lesson for all future generations (see Num 25:1-5; Deut 4:3; Hos 9:10).

Like the Canaanites, the patriarchs addressed God as *El* (an abbreviation for "God"), but never as Baal. *El* usually appears in combination with certain other names. These include *El Olam*, "Everlasting God" (Gen 21:33); *El Elyon*, "God Most High" (14:18-22); *El Elohe Israel*, "God, the God of Israel" (33:20); *El Roeh*, "God Who Sees" (16:13); *El Shaddai*, "God Almighty," or "God of the Mountain" (17:1; see Exod 6:3); and *El Bethel*, "God of Bethel." Most of these titles were associated with a particular place of worship established by the patriarchs in the land of Canaan.

According to Exodus 6:2-3, God was revealed to Moses as *Yahweh*, always rendered in English versions of the Bible as "the LORD." The God who appeared to Moses as *Yahweh* ("the LORD") was the One who had appeared to Abraham, Isaac, and Jacob as *El Shaddai*, "God Almighty."

There were few priests in the patriarchal period (see Gen 14:18), and every father could offer sacrifices on behalf of his household (see 22:13; 31:54; 46:1). It was permissible to erect an altar in any place where a revelation of God had occurred (see 12:7f.; 13:18; 26:25; 35:7). Prayer was a vital part of worship, though prayer in this period is usually depicted as a normal conversation with God. Prayer also included intercession on behalf of others (18:22-33; 20:7, 17). It was only when worship became more of a public exercise that singing became a part of it.

Prominent Themes

As we work our way through the patriarchal narratives, we may note certain recurring themes. Prominent among these is the theme of *promise*.[4] God made the following promises to Abraham and his descendants:

- the promise of a son for the present and a multitude of descendants for the future (15:1-5; 16:10; 18:10; 22:17; 26:1-5; 28:13-14)
- the promise of a land to possess (12:14-17; 15:7-21; 28:4; 35:12; 48:1-3; 50:24)
- the promise of blessing, involving all nations and all peoples of the earth (12:2-3; 17:16; 28:13-14)
- the promise of a covenant (15:18-21; 17:1-8)
- the promise of God's continuing presence throughout life's journey (12:1; 28:15, 20-22; 31:3; 39:2, 21; 46:1-4; 48:15-16, 21)
- the promise of dominion (27:29; 37:5-10; 41:42-43; 42:6; 43:26-28; 49:8)

The second theme is that of *election*, involving the paradoxical choice of a younger son in the family instead of the firstborn. Isaac was chosen over Ishmael (17:15-21; 21:8-14), Jacob over Esau (25:19-23; 27:18-29), Joseph over the firstborn Reuben (37:5-11), Perez over Zerah (38:27-30; see Ruth 4:18-20), Ephraim over Manasseh (48:8-19), and Judah over Reuben (49:8-12). It was an early instance of the first being last and the last being first.

The third theme to be noted is that of *conflict*, both family and territorial. Family conflict occurred between husband and wife (3:12;

16:5; 27:1-17; 30:1-2), between wife and wife (16:4-6; 30:1-24), between parent and child (37:29-35), and between other relatives (13:5-7; 31:1-16). Territorial conflict occurred between Abraham and Lot (13:5-13), between Abraham and Abimelech (21:22-32) and between Isaac and Abimelech (26:18-33).[5] Territorial conflicts seem to have been easier to resolve than family conflicts.

Abraham and Sarah

Almost half the book of Genesis is about Abraham and Sarah. No other persons receive so much attention. Of all the characters in the Bible, Abraham alone came to be known as "the friend of God" (2 Chron 20:7; Isa 41:8; Jas 2:23). Living in the midst of a pagan culture, Abraham and Sarah caught a vision of a better world. They set out in search of that world with no security but the promise of God. It is no accident that they are mentioned so prominently in the roll call of the faithful in the book of Hebrews (Heb 11:8-12, 17-19).

Claus Westermann[6] notes that the history of God's dealings with God's people in the Hebrew Scriptures has three important turning points: (1) at the beginning of the patriarchal history (Gen 12), (2) at the beginning of Israel's history as a nation (Exod 1), and (3) at the beginning of the history of the kings (1 Sam 1). Westermann also notes that at each of these important junctures in biblical history there is an extended birth narrative, detailing in succession the births of Isaac, Moses, and Samuel. Taken together, they suggest that all of God's great acts in history begin with the birth of a child. The New Testament is also prefaced with a remarkable birth narrative, and once again a mother sings her hymn of praise.

God's initial call to Abraham (12:1-3) is set against the background of the revolt of the nations on the plain of Shinar (11:1-9). There the building of a city and its tower had resulted in the scattering of the nations and the confusion of their languages. But God had not given up on the nations or abandoned them to their fate. Abraham's call was God's act of redeeming grace toward the nations, for through Abraham and his descendants all nations were to be blessed. This was the initial act in God's great drama of redemption, a drama that reached its climax in the incarnation, death, and resurrection of Jesus Christ.

Hebrews 11:8 describes Abraham's response to God's call in these words, "By faith Abraham obeyed when he was called to set out for a place that he was to receive as an inheritance; and he set out, not knowing where he was going." Three things added to the difficulty of Abraham's decision: the barrenness of Sarah, the uncertainty as to his destination, and the occupation of the land by the Canaanites. Common sense would have ruled out such a journey as he was about to under-take, but common sense was overruled by an uncommon faith.

Faith on Trial

Abraham's faith did not spring forth full-grown but had to be nurtured and refined in the trials and fortunes of life. His robust response at the beginning was followed by other occasions on which fear overcame him, and he showed an almost total lack of faith. Although he was fundamentally committed to God's will for his life, he sometimes acted as if God's promises could not be trusted. Sin is born of doubt and nurtured by anxiety, and Abraham was certainly not immune to its onslaught. Over and over again God had to rescue him from embar-rassing situations that he had created for himself.

There is an early rabbinic tradition that Abraham's faith was tested on ten separate occasions during his lifetime. The list that follows has been garnered from various sources and adapted for our own use.

(1) *The call to leave family and homeland* (12:1-3). Abraham's call specified three things he must leave behind, and they seem to have been deliberately placed in ascending order. The three were his country, his relatives, and finally his immediate family. Each phase in the separation became more personal and, therefore, more painful. The impression we get of Abraham here and throughout the Genesis account is of someone who was always being called on to give up something he treasured, whether the security of familiar surroundings, country, kinsmen and family, or, as in the supreme test of his faith, his son Isaac (chap. 22).

In our highly mobile society we are more or less accustomed to being uprooted and separated from home and loved ones. In Abra-ham's day, however, the only real security people knew was that provided by family ties. Peace, security, blessing, and well-being had their source in one's tribe, clan, or family. When people left this safe zone, they were exposed to all kinds of danger. Gerhard von Rad wrote that "to leave home and to break ancestral bonds was to expect of ancient men [and women] almost the impossible."[7]

As noted above, Abraham passed the first test of his faith in a commendable way. His example reminds me of something said by a professor of political science at the college where one of our daughters was studying. He told his students that a true philosopher was someone who was always open to new truth, never too attached to material things, and never too dependent on familiar things. We wouldn't be too far afield to apply these same qualifications to Abraham.

(2) *Famine in Canaan and flight to Egypt* (12:10–13:1). The second test occurred soon after Abraham and Sarah arrived in Canaan. They discovered that the land was in the grip of a severe famine (12:10). What a disconcerting development! Abraham and Sarah had left behind the well-watered plains of Mesopotamia, and what had they gotten in return? A promised land that was subject to periodic droughts! What kind of trade was that?

Abraham saw no way out except to take refuge in Egypt. That was what people of the Middle East usually did in times of famine (see 41:5; 43:1-2; 47:4). Egypt was not as susceptible to crop failure as its neighbors, for its harvests depended not upon the changing seasons but on the annual rise and fall of the Nile River.

In making his decision to abandon the promised land, Abraham apparently did not take time to inquire of the Lord. It had been easier for him to let go of his life than to trust God for daily bread. As Abraham faced famine, he saw only two alternatives: he could either remain in Canaan and risk starvation, or go to Egypt where food was plentiful. It apparently had not occurred to him that there might be a third alternative, namely, that of remaining in Canaan and trusting God to provide a way out. Abraham had yet to learn that God could do the seemingly impossible (see 18:13-14a).

When Abraham and Sarah arrived in Egypt, their situation worsened. Fearful of what the Egyptians might do to him when they saw the beauty of Sarah, Abraham conspired with her to tell the Egyptians that she was his sister. But while this was true (see 20:12), it was only a half-truth. And while it worked for Abraham, it jeopardized Sarah and the entire future of the Hebrew people. Abraham had been willing to sacrifice Sarah in order to save his own skin. The outcome might have been disastrous if God had not stepped in. This was but one of several occasions reported in Genesis when God had to overrule the failures and weaknesses of the people in order to achieve the divine purpose in history (see 45:5-8; 50:20).

(3) *Conflict between the herdsmen of Abraham and Lot* (13:2-18). Having been left an orphan early in life (11:27-28), Lot was cared for at first by his grandfather Terah (11:31) and later by his uncle Abraham (12:4). The early ties between Abraham and Lot seem to have been very close, for Abraham addressed him as his brother, or kinsman (13:8; see also 14:16), and treated him as if he were his own son.

Lot had evidently accompanied Abraham on the journey to Egypt, since they were together on the return trip (13:1). As it happens so often in family situations, it was the increase of wealth that led to quarreling and eventual separation between the two. Abraham could be described upon his return from Egypt as "very rich in livestock, in silver, and in gold" (13:2), while it could be said of Lot that he "had flocks and herds and tents" (13:5). Grazing land was scarce in the hill country of Canaan, and the herdsmen of the two men found it difficult to coexist in the same limited area.

Abraham undertook to resolve the crisis before it got out of hand. While he had the authority as head of his clan to order his nephew to leave at once, he chose instead to come to him with a reconciling proposition. He took Lot to a lookout point between the lush Jordan valley to the east and the rugged hill country to the west and asked him to choose the one he preferred. Abraham would then take the other as his inheritance.

There was never any doubt about which portion Lot would choose. He seems to have been programmed to make every decision on the basis of what was in it for himself. He chose the well-watered valley of the Jordan because he thought it was the better bargain. He was willing to part company with one of the greatest men who ever lived in order to own a little river-bottom land. Little did he suspect that his choice was the beginning of his troubles and that he would never escape the need for Abraham's protection or his intercession.

God honored Abraham's nobility of character and unselfishness of choice by renewing the promise to give this land to him and his descendants in perpetuity (13:14-17). Lot's departure meant that Abraham had finally broken all ties to his father's house and was ready to begin a new phase of his life. What had seemed like a sacrifice on his part turned out to be a blessing in disguise.

(4) *Invasion of the land of Canaan; Abraham's mission to rescue Lot* (14:1-24). This is the first biblical record of warfare between nations. It involved a confederacy of four kings from the Mesopotamian region in the far north who attacked five Canaanite kings who were their vassals and whose small city-states were located south of the Dead Sea (14:1-2). It seems that the Canaanite kings had rebelled against their Mesopotamian overlords and had suffered an invasion as punishment for their rebellion. The invaders, led by one of their number, named Chedorlaomer, quickly overran the Canaanite city-states, looted their cities, captured their kings, and took some of their citizens as hostages (14:3-12). Included among the cities was Sodom, and Lot and his family were among those taken as prisoners of war.

As soon as news of the invasion reached Abraham, he mobilized 318 of his trained warriors and set out in hot pursuit (14:13-16). He caught up with the invaders at the Canaanite border near Dan and pursued them as far north as the vicinity of Damascus before defeating them and securing the release of their prisoners, including Lot's family. He also took back the booty seized from Sodom and the other Canaanite cities.

As Abraham was returning home, he came near Salem (later called Jerusalem) and was met by two kings: Bera, the king of Sodom, and Melchizedek, the king of Salem. Melchizedek had come out to offer Abraham bread and wine and to bless him in the name of *El Elyon*, "God Most High" (14:18-20). As an expression of his gratitude, Abraham offered Melchizedek a tithe of all the spoils he had brought back from the battlefield.

Bera, the king of Sodom, was emboldened by this exchange to make Abraham a proposition. He said, "Give me the persons [prisoners of war], but take the goods [booty] for yourself" (14:21). Abraham was immediately suspicious of Bera's motive. Abraham had not hesitated to accept the gift of food and drink from Melchizedek, since there were no strings attached. But to have accepted the generous offer of Bera would have put the patriarch forever in his debt. A wise person knows how to strike a balance between dependence and independence, when to accept a gift, and when to reject it. Abraham was unwilling to sacrifice his freedom for the sake of personal gain.

(5) *Delay in the promised gift of a son* (15:1-6; 16:1-4). Abraham had no sooner returned victorious from the field of battle (14:13-16) and from his encounter with the king of Sodom (14:21-24) than doubts about his own future plunged him into a state of spiritual depression. We find him saying, "O Lord God, what wilt you give me, for I continue childless, and the heir of my house is my servant Eliezer of Damascus?" (15:2). This could be paraphrased to read, "O Lord God, what good are any of your gifts to me so long as I remain childless and my only hope for an heir is my servant Eliezer of Damascus?" Elsewhere in the Bible it is the barren mother who grieves because she has not been able to conceive (see Gen 30:1; 1 Sam 1:1-18), but here it is the childless father who laments his future without an heir.

God responded to Abraham's fears in a gracious manner. First, God assured him that a son yet to be born would become his heir, and not Eliezer of Damascus (15:4). Then God took Abraham out under the Canaanite sky and gave him a lesson in astronomy. God told him to count the stars, if he could, for like the number of the stars so would be the number of his descendants (15:5; see also Deut 1:10; 10:22).

Abraham was convinced by the words of assurance God had spoken. We are told that Abraham "believed the Lord; and the Lord reckoned it to him as righteousness" (15:6). Many judge this verse to contain the most theologically significant statement in Genesis, if not in the entirety of the Hebrew Scriptures. Taken as a whole, the verse teaches that Abraham's act of faith assured his acceptance by God as a righteous person. Instead of trying to work out his future by his own manipulative efforts, he had decided to let God take control. Verse 7, in combination with Habakkuk 2:4b, became the cornerstone of Paul's doctrine of justification by faith (see Rom 4:3, 9, 22; Gal 3:6). It also became the battle cry of Martin Luther's Reformation in the sixteenth century A.D.

The events described in Genesis 16:1-4 suggest that the faith of Sarah may not have kept pace with that of her husband. As one carrying the stigma of barrenness, Sarah was fretting over the delay in the birth of a son, although Abraham seems to have come to terms with it (15:1-7). Sarah had devised a plan whereby her Egyptian hand-maid, Hagar, would be given to Abraham as a surrogate wife. Any children born to this union would be considered the children of Sarah, thus removing her stigma of childlessness. Sarah's plan worked much as she had anticipated, and in due time Hagar became pregnant with Abraham's child (16:3-4). At this point, however, relations between Sarah and her handmaid began to go sour (16:4b). Sarah discovered that living under the same roof with a woman married to her husband created more problems than it solved. Friction between the two women eventually grew so sharp that it produced a fresh trial of faith for Abraham.

(6) *Command for Abraham to be circumcised at age ninety-nine* (17:1-27). Ancient rabbis listed the command for Abraham to be circumcised at age ninety-nine as one of the tests of his faith. Chapter 17 gives a detailed account of God's covenant with the patriarch, which should be compared with the parallel account in 15:7-21. The sign of the Abrahamic covenant was circumcision, just as the rainbow had been the sign of the earlier covenant with Noah (9:12-16).

God was introduced on this solemn occasion as *El Shaddai*, "God Almighty," or "God of the Mountain" (17:1). Wherever this name occurs, it emphasizes the blessings and protection coming from God (17:2; 28:3; 35:11; 43:14; 48:3; 49:25). The blessing extended to Abraham on this occasion was a reaffirmation of that given to him at the time of his call (17:2-8; 12:1-3).

The most remarkable feature of the Abrahamic covenant is its demand that all male members of the covenant community be circumcised (17:9-14; see Jer 4:4). Circumcision was not invented by the Hebrews but was already being practiced by many of their neighbors, including Egyptians, Canaanites, Edomites, Ammonites, and Moabites (Jer 9:25-26). No one knows the origin of the practice or its original significance. But whatever its meaning in other cultures, to the Israelites it served as a sign and seal of the covenant. It was as if God's covenant were actually present in the flesh of the circumcised male (17:13). The requirement was so binding that any male who had not been circumcised could not participate as a member of the covenant community (17:14). Abraham's response to the call to be circumcised is described in 17:22-27. His advanced age was not allowed to be an impediment to his obedience.

(7) *Conflict with Abimelech* (20:1-18). Gerar was a small desert kingdom located south of Beersheba and ruled over by a king named Abimelech. For reasons not explained in the text, Abraham chose to leave his place of residence at Mamre (18:1) and move to Gerar (20:1). When he got to Gerar, he reported that Sarah was not his wife but his sister (20:2a), much as he had done earlier in Egypt (12:10-13). What prompted the patriarch to tell the same lie twice? Was he not able to learn from his own mistakes? The reason Abraham gave to Abimelech for his lapse of character is found in verse 11: "I did it because I thought, There is no fear of God at all in this place, and they will kill me because of my wife."

Perhaps it was the patriarch himself who was lacking in the fear of God. At any rate, he was willing to expose Sarah to great danger without even asking her permission. Almost to the end of his life, Abraham continued the zigzag course of obedience and disobedience that had characterized him from the start.

(8) *The expulsion of Hagar and Ishmael* (21:8-21). The birth of Isaac is told almost as if it were a normal occurrence (21:1-2). He was named Isaac (21:3), according to the instructions previously given to his father (17:19), and he was the only one of the three great patriarchs who did not undergo a later change of name.

We know, of course, that there was nothing normal about the twenty-five-year gap between the call of Abraham and the birth of Isaac (see 12:4; 21:5). When the birth finally took place, the parents were too old to do much celebrating. We are told that when Isaac was old enough to be weaned, perhaps around his third or fourth birthday, Abraham made a great feast (21:8). Weaning was considered a significant rite of passage in the life of a child in biblical times (see 1 Sam 1:22-24; 1 Kgs 11:20). It is still an occasion for celebration in cultures where infant mortality rates are high.

Things went well at Isaac's weaning party until Sarah happened to see Hagar's son Ishmael playing with (or mocking) her son Isaac (21:9). For reasons not explained in the text, this infuriated Sarah, and she demanded of Abraham that he drive out the slave woman and her son (21:10).

This demand placed Abraham in a quandary. He loved Isaac, to be sure, but he also loved Ishmael, and Abraham found it painful to drive

Ishmael away from home. His dilemma is expressed in verse 11: "The matter was very distressing to Abraham on account of his son."

God came to Abraham's rescue by telling him it was all right to honor Sarah's request. God also promised Abraham that Ishmael would become the father of a great nation since he, too, was Abraham's offspring (21:13). Verse 14 describes how Abraham rose early in the morning, provided bread and water for the journey, and sent Hagar and Ishmael on their way. Abraham's silence during these preparations speaks more eloquently than words. Already the reader is being prepared for another early morning rising for a journey involving Abraham and his other son (22:3).

There is an ironic twist worthy of note in the account of Hagar's expulsion from Abraham's household. It is likely that Hagar, who was the ancestress of the Ishmaelites, was part of Pharaoh's earlier gift to Abraham and Sarah (12:16). If so, Hagar had been taken out of Egypt without having any choice in the matter. Years later, it would be Ishmaelite traders, descendants of Hagar, who would take Joseph to Egypt against his will and sell him to Potiphar (37:23-28). The reversal of roles between the Hebrews and the Ishmaelites is intriguing.

In the story of Hagar's flight with Ishmael, we have convincing evidence that God does not abandon the weak and suffering of this world. God heard the cry of a little slave boy dying of thirst in the desert and provided water for him to drink (21:15-21). God also heard the cry of little Moses centuries later when he was set adrift in his tiny ark of bulrushes on the River Nile (Exod 2:6). One slave child was saved from thirst and the other from drowning, and in neither case did God check the color of their skin before acting. In one instance God saved an Egyptian child from Israelite oppression, while in the other it was an Israelite child who was saved from Egyptian oppression. Whenever oppression occurs today, regardless of whom the oppressor may be, God still takes the side of the oppressed and still insists that justice become the accepted standard in human relations (see Isa 1:16-17; 58:6-7; Amos 5:24; Matt 25:34-40; Jas 1:27).

(9) *The sacrifice of Isaac* (22:1-19). This episode in the life of Abraham is known in Jewish circles as the *Akedah*, or "The Binding of Isaac." It was the supreme test of the patriarch's faith. There is a parallel between the wording of the call to offer his son and the earlier call for Abraham to begin his pilgrimage of faith. In both instances he was commanded simply to go to a place that God would show him (12:1; 22:12). The two calls differ in that the first required that Abraham cut himself off from his past and the second that he surrender his future. The similarity between the two calls is further

revealed in Abraham's response: in both instances he obeyed without delay or equivocation.

The call to sacrifice Isaac apparently came to Abraham at night, for we are told that he rose early in the morning, made the necessary preparations, and set out on his journey (22:3). The next three days are passed over in silence, although Abraham's resolution must have been tested every step of the way. He loved Isaac, as God gently reminded him (22:2), but he also loved God. While both loves were legitimate, the latter outweighed the former.

Arriving at the mount of sacrifice, Abraham separated himself from his servants. What he had to do now he must do alone. So far as he knew, Isaac must indeed be offered as a sacrifice upon this mountain. Father and son ascended in silence, until the son's inquisitiveness got the best of him. "Father," he said, "The fire and the wood are here, but where is the lamb for a burnt offering?" And all Abraham could manage in response was, "God will provide the lamb for a burnt offering, my son."

At the mountaintop Abraham built an altar of loose stones, laid the wood in order upon the altar, bound Isaac's hands and feet, and laid him upon the wood. Then he raised his slaughter knife in preparation for the sacrifice. At the climatic moment, however, a voice from heaven stopped him, "Do not lay your hand on the boy or do anything to him; for now I know . . ." Abraham had passed the most crucial test of his entire career. From that moment onward he was known as "the friend of God," a title bestowed upon no other human being (see Isa 41:8).

(10) *The death and burial of Sarah* (23:1-20). The last trial Abraham faced was the death and burial of Sarah. This trial was even more severe because Abraham was in a foreign land and his friends and relatives were miles away. I know firsthand his feelings, for Vernice and I lost an infant daughter while living in Brazil, and we missed our family more at that time than at any other.

It is regrettable that we do not have more information about Sarah and the part she played in the momentous events that took place during her lifetime. The culture of her day dictated that she live always in the shadow of her husband, although her gifts and talents probably were equal to his. She, like Abraham, received a change of name, a special sign of divine favor (17:15). Both she and Abraham were guilty of occasional lapses of faith and unkind behavior toward others, but Sarah seems to have been judged more severely than Abraham. For instance, both laughed when told that they would be given a son in their old age (17:17; 18:12), but only Sarah was reprimanded for her lack of faith (18:13-15). Twice she was allowed to be shut up in a foreign king's harem, just to protect Abraham's life, but, when the danger had passed, only he received gifts to compensate for his trouble. It had not been easy for Sarah to be married to this "wandering Aramean."

Perhaps the most difficult occasion of all was the near sacrifice of her only son Isaac, although her name is not even mentioned in the account. Early Jewish rabbis reported that Abraham hid the true purpose of his journey to the land of Moriah from Sarah lest she try to hinder his going. There is no mention in the Bible of Isaac's having returned home with Abraham after the dramatic events at the mountain (22:19). There is a Jewish legend that when Sarah saw Abraham returning alone, she surmised that Isaac had indeed been sacrificed, whereupon she was stricken with grief and died soon afterward.

According to information given in 17:17 and 21:5, Sarah was 90 years old when Isaac was born. Elsewhere we are told that she was 127 at the time of her death (23:1), which would have made Isaac 37 years old at the time. He was married to Rebecca three years later (25:20), which helps to explain the statement that his marriage provided comfort for him after his mother's death (24:67).

The Bible doesn't record anyone's death and burial arrangements before chapter 23 of Genesis. Up until this time Abraham had not made any plans for securing a family burial plot in the land of Canaan. Now he was obliged to do so, even in the midst of his grief over the death of his companion (23:1-20). The pilgrimage he and Sarah had made had been long in years as well as in miles. It had taken them from their pagan roots in Ur to a new covenant relationship with God in the land of Canaan. Their obedience earned them a place of honor among the heroes of faith listed in Hebrews 11.

Abraham's purchase of the Cave of Machpelah from Ephron the Hittite provides a classic example of Oriental "haggling," always performed behind a screen of politeness. Abraham was at a distinct disadvantage both because he was a foreigner and because he felt obliged to conclude a deal at whatever cost. This is why Ephron offered the land at several times its value. He asked 400 shekels of silver for a nondescript cave, a small parcel of land, and a few trees. Centuries later, Jeremiah bought his cousin's field in Anathoth, a much more fertile section of the country, for only seventeen shekels of silver (Jer 32:9).

Abraham's efforts to secure a resting place for Sarah are indicative of the great respect for the dead and of the significance of the proper burial of the dead that continue to characterize the Jewish faith to this day. The purchase of a burial place in the land of Canaan also gave Abraham clear title to a small part of the Holy Land. It reflected Abraham's certainty that God would someday fulfill the promise to give the entire land to him and his descendants.

Conclusion

The story of Abraham quickly comes to a close after the burial of Sarah. Having performed his responsibility to the dead, Abraham quickly turned his attention to the needs of the living. He must send his servant back to Haran to secure a wife for Isaac from among his own kindred, lest Isaac intermarry with the pagan women of Canaan. The story of the servant's successful mission is told in exquisite detail in chapter 24. It rivals any nonbiblical love story that has ever been told.

When this task had been accomplished, the Bible tells us, "Abraham breathed his last and died in a good old age, an old man and full of years, and was gathered to his people" (25:8). He was laid to rest beside Sarah in the cave of Machpelah (25:9-10).

Notes

[1]Martha A. Morrison, "Nuzi," in *Anchor Bible Dictionary*, ed. David Noel Freedman (New York: Doubleday, 1992) 4:1156-62.

[2]W. F. Albright, *Yahweh and the Gods of Canaan* (Garden City NY: Doubleday, 1968)110- 52.

[3]Marguerite Yon, D. Pardee, and Pierre Bordreuil, "Ugarit," in *Anchor Bible Dictionary*, ed. David Noel Freedman (New York: Doubleday, 1992) 6:695-721.

[4]See Claus Westermann, *The Promises to the Fathers*, trans. David E. Green (Philadelphia: Press, 1980) 132-63.

[5]See Devora Steinmetz, *From Father to Son: Kinship, Conflict, and Continuity in Genesis* (Louisville KY: Westminster/John Knox Press, 1991).

[6]Claus Westermann, *A Thousand Years and a Day* (Philadelphia: Fortress Press, 1962) 118f.

[7]Gerhard von Rad, *Genesis*, trans. John H. Marks (London: SCM Press Ltd, 1956) 157.

For Further Reading

Alter, Robert. *The Art of Biblical Narrative*. New York: Basic Books, 1981.

Fox, Everett. *The Five Books of Moses*. New York: Schocken Books, 1995.

Kelley, Page. *Discovering Genesis 1–24*. Carmel NY: Guideposts, 1987.

Sarna, Nahum M. "Genesis." In *The J.P.S Torah Commentary*, 3-87. Philadelphia: The Jewish Publication Society, 1989.

Chapter 3

Heirs of the Promise
Genesis 25:12–50:26

The descendants of Abraham inherited the twofold promise of land and descendants. The last half of Genesis traces the passing on of this promise to successive generations through Isaac, Jacob, and the sons of Jacob, particularly Joseph and Judah. The transfer of the promise from Abraham to Isaac was fairly simple, since Isaac was an only son. The situation changed, however, when there was more than one potential recipient of the promise, as was the case with Jacob and Esau and later with the twelve sons of Jacob. In both instances the stage was set for strife and contention over which of the sons would inherit the promise and receive the father's blessing.

Isaac and Rebekah

All we know about the middle years of Isaac's life is found in Genesis 26. Other references to him concern either his youth or his old age. Following Abraham's death we might have expected attention to be focused on Isaac for some time to come, but, instead, it shifts almost immediately from him to his children, especially Jacob.

Isaac was the child of his parents' old age and seems to have been overprotected in his youth (see 21:8-10). He gives the impression of having been withdrawn and perhaps somewhat insecure. When Abraham was ready to sacrifice Isaac, there is no indication that he even raised his voice in protest (22:10-11). And when Abraham decided to procure a wife for Isaac, he entrusted the task of finding her not to Isaac, himself, but to an unnamed servant (24:2-4), even though Isaac was already forty years of age (25:19-20). It was fortunate that the wife obtained for him turned out to be aggressive and resourceful. It has even been suggested that the introverted Isaac saw in her a "mother substitute" (see 24:67).

Among the few facts we know about Isaac's life, the following are worthy of note. He, like Abraham before him, was the father of two nations, Israel and Edom. Both he and Abraham were married to barren women (25:21-23), and both had to wait many years for an heir to be born (25:26). Through all their delay, however, Isaac and Rebekah seem to have maintained their faith in God's promise and in the power of prayer (25:21). Isaac was the only patriarch to remain monogamous all his life and the only one never to have left the promised land. He was also the first to settle down and to begin to farm the land (26:12).

Most of chapter 26 deals with events that took place while Isaac was residing in Gerar in the southern part of Canaan. Abraham had also lived there for a brief time several years earlier (20:1-18). Just as Abraham had done previously, Isaac lied to the king of Gerar about his wife, saying she was only his sister (26:6-11). This time, however, the lie was discovered before Rebekah's safety was threatened, and the king avoided having to give gifts to Isaac.

Isaac proceeded to redig the wells that Abraham had dug before him, but that had been filled in by the Philistines (26:18). Isaac also gave the wells the same names that his father had given them. When the herdsmen of Gerar challenged Isaac's right to the wells, he simply moved further away and dug another well (26:19-22). He was at heart a peacemaker, although he seems to have been more successful at handling conflict with his neighbors than with the members of his own household.

The first recorded self-revelation of God to Isaac occurred while he was in the land of Gerar. A famine had driven him there, and he was apparently toying with the idea of traveling on to Egypt, as Abraham had done when the first famine struck (12:10). This was the point at which the Lord intervened and told Isaac not to go to Egypt but to continue to sojourn in the land of Canaan so that he might inherit the promises given to his father Abraham (26:2-5). Isaac was soon able to move back to Beersheba, where the Lord appeared to him once more and reaffirmed the promises given to him in Gerar (26:23-24). To celebrate this momentous occasion, Isaac built an altar, called upon the name of the Lord, and put down stakes in this hallowed place (26:25).

How can we describe Isaac's role in sacred history? First, Isaac deserves to be remembered as a peacemaker. In an age characterized by force and aggression, he chose to follow a course of nonaggression and of appeal to reason. It probably made him appear to be cowardly at times, but in the end it enabled him to make peace with his enemies and thereby insure the safety of his family. Second, Isaac remained loyal to the tradition he had received from his parents and handed it on to future generations. A modern Jewish writer expressed Isaac's role as a keeper of the tradition in these words.

> After the revolutionary and often stormy experiences of his father, the son's life becomes the necessary halting place where new religious insights are absorbed and incorporated into patterns of thought and deed. Isaac is the bridge between Abraham and Jacob, the essential link in the chain of greatness.[1]

Jacob, Rachel, and Leah

The story of the life of Jacob is like a drama in four acts. The first act has its setting in Canaan and covers the period from Jacob's birth until his flight from Esau (25:19–28:22). The second act is set in Paddan-Aram and describes the years Jacob spent in the household of Laban (29:1–32:2). The third act extends from the time of Jacob's return to Canaan until the death and burial of his father (32:3–34:29). The record of the fourth act is interwoven with the Joseph narratives (37; 42:1-5; 43:1-15; 45:12–50:14). It tells of Jacob's favoritism toward Joseph, of Joseph's being sold into slavery, of Jacob's sons being sent to Egypt for food, of Jacob's own migration to Egypt, of his death in Egypt, and of his burial in the cave of Machpelah.

The Story of Two Brothers

Jacob's life was bound up with that of his twin brother Esau. These two were born when Isaac and Rebekah had been married for twenty years (25:20, 26). This story illustrates how conflict that is not handled properly may become the controlling factor in a family's life. The conflict between these two brothers was aggravated by the favoritism that Isaac showed toward Esau and that Rebekah showed toward Jacob. One writer has observed that each of the sons was only half-loved. Children deserve something better from their parents than this.

The brothers grew up with widely differing lifestyles. Esau was a simple man who loved the outdoors. He secured his food through the uncertain means of hunting. He seems to have been a thoroughgoing materialist, interested only in satisfying his physical appetites and passions. Whenever he wanted something, he wanted it immediately. His impulsiveness caused him to sell his birthright (the privileged inheritance rights of the firstborn) to Jacob for a bowl of lentil stew (25:29-34). This rash act caused him to be remembered as a person lacking in spiritual sensitivity (Heb 12:16-17). It would have been difficult for the patriarchal blessing to be transmitted to future generations through one whose vision was so limited.

Of course, Jacob was not all that saintly when he first appeared on the stage of history. He had already learned how to manipulate people and circumstances to his own advantage. He lived by the motto that "God helps those who help themselves." He shrewdly bargained for his brother's birthright. He deceived his blind father and stole his brother's blessing without asking nice questions of conscience. He had mastered the art of deception.

God did not choose Jacob because of what he was but because of what he was capable of becoming. He was the type of person who

possessed the potential both for great good and great evil. Two opposite forces within him were always struggling for mastery. If his
selfish, deceitful nature had prevailed, he would have been a curse to
those around him, but, because the spiritual side of his character eventually prevailed, he became a blessing to all future generations. This is
why God chose to be identified as "the God of Abraham, the God of
Isaac, and *the God of Jacob*" (italics mine).

The Passing of the Blessing

When Rebekah became pregnant with twins, God promised that Jacob
would rule over Esau, although Esau was to be the older of the two.
However, even this promise failed to give Rebekah the assurance she
needed. When the boys were grown and it looked as if Isaac was about
to pass the patriarchal blessing to Esau, she decided to take matters
into her own hands.

The account of what transpired as a result of her decision is found
in Genesis 27:1–28:5. This is a story of family conflict vividly
described in seven scenes. The story consists almost entirely of
dialogue. All four family members participate in the dialogue. The
speaking pairs in the order of their appearance are Isaac and Esau
(27:1-4), Rebekah and Jacob (27:5-17), Isaac and Jacob (27:18-29),
Isaac and Esau (27:30-41), Rebekah and Jacob (27:42-45), Rebekah
and Isaac (27:46), and Isaac and Jacob (28:1-5). (An innovative way to
present this biblical story to a class would be to select five capable
speakers, four to read the speeches of the family members in the
shifting scenes and one to serve as narrator, reading the narrative
sections that tie the speeches together.)

Jacob's Encounter with God

When Esau returned from the hunt and discovered that his brother
had stolen his blessing, he vowed to kill him as soon as their father
was dead (27:41). This prompted Rebekah to try to convince Jacob to
flee to Haran and to seek safety with her family (27:42-45). After
securing his father's consent and blessing, Jacob set out on his journey
(28:1-5).

Nightfall overtook Jacob when he was several miles north of his
home, and he was obliged to make camp in a strange place (28:10-11).
As he slept that night, Jacob dreamed of a stairway stretching from
heaven to earth with angels ascending and descending upon it (28:12).
In his dream he also saw the Lord standing above the stairway to
deliver a blessing to Jacob (28:13-14), the same blessing the Lord had
earlier bestowed upon Abraham (17:3-8) and Isaac (26:3-5). The Lord

also promised to accompany Jacob on his journey to Haran and to return him safely to his home in Canaan (28:15).

Jacob awakened from his dream, startled to realize that he had seen the Lord in this lonely place, and grateful that the Lord had spoken to him in such a gracious way. To commemorate the occasion, he set up a stone, anointed it with oil, and named the place Bethel, "House of God" (28:18-19). He then vowed that if God would indeed go with him to Haran, supply his needs, bring him safely back to Canaan, and consent to be his God, then the stone Jacob had set up would become God's sanctuary, and he would offer the tithe of all that God would give him (28:20-22).[2]

Some have criticized Jacob's vow as an attempt to drive a hard bargain with God, but this seems to be an unfair criticism. After all, this was only the first step in Jacob's pilgrimage of faith and the beginning of his commitment to the God of his ancestors. We sometimes forget that God relates to those who are beginning their pilgrimage of faith on the basis of individual comprehension. Certainly Jacob was not spiritually mature, but God had not finished with him. "Jacob" would not become "Israel" until he had been to Haran and back (32:27-28). He still had before him many years of discipline, chastisement, and purification by affliction.

Jacob in Haran

Jacob journeyed northward from Bethel and arrived near the city of Haran late one afternoon, about the time local shepherds were gathering at a community well to water their flocks before bedding down for the night. This set the stage for Jacob's first encounter with Rachel, who had come to the well to water her father's flock. This entire episode is written in literary form known as "a betrothal type-scene." The features of this literary form are best described by Alter:

> The betrothal type-scene, then, must take place with the future bridegroom, or his surrogate, having journeyed to a foreign land. There he encounters a girl—at a well. Someone, either the man or the girl, then draws water from the well; afterward, the girl rushes to bring home the news of the stranger's arrival (the verbs "hurry" and "run" are given recurrent emphasis at this juncture of the type-scene); finally, a betrothal is concluded between the stranger and the girl, in the majority of instances, only after he has been invited to a meal.[3]

This literary form is also found in the story of Isaac's betrothal to Rebekah (Gen 24:10-61) and in the story of Moses' betrothal to Zipporah (Exod 2:15b-22).

Jacob spent the next twenty years as a member of Laban's household. During fourteen of those years he worked without pay in order to be granted permission to marry Laban's daughters (29:20, 30). Afterwards he continued to serve as a contract shepherd for his father-in-law. The two men were actually so much alike that neither could tolerate the other. They were fiercely competitive in all their business dealings, although Jacob usually managed to come out ahead of Laban. Jacob also faced conflict within his immediate family. Rachel and Leah were constantly vying for his favor, and they used their handmaids as pawns in this love game. This resulted in the birth of twelve sons, from whom the twelve tribes of Israel later received their names. The following list, based on Genesis 29:31–30:24 and 35:16-20, shows the order in which they were born and the mother of each.

(1) Reuben (Leah)
(2) Simeon (Leah)
(3) Levi (Leah)
(4) Judah (Leah)
(5) Dan (Bilhah, Rachel's handmaid)
(6) Naphtali (Bilhah)
(7) Gad (Zilpah, Leah's handmaid)
(8) Asher (Zilpah)
(9) Issachar (Leah)
(10) Zebulun (Leah)
(11) Joseph (Rachel)
(12) Benjamin (Rachel)

The tribe of Simeon seems to have dropped out at an early date (see Deut 33:6-25), and its place was filled by the creation of two Joseph tribes, Manasseh and Ephraim (Gen 46:20).

The rivalry between Jacob and Laban eventually became so bitter that Jacob feared for his life. Taking advantage of Laban's absence from home during the sheep-shearing season, Jacob gathered his family and flocks and fled toward Canaan (31:19-21). When news of this reached Laban, Jacob already had a head start, and it took Laban a week to overtake him (31:22-23). Laban would likely have harmed Jacob if God had not warned him against doing so (31:29). Laban's chief complaint was that Jacob had stolen his household gods (31:30). Jacob vehemently denied the charge, unaware that Rachel had indeed taken her father's gods when she left Haran. Jacob offered to let Laban conduct a tent-to-tent search, with the understanding that anyone found with the gods should be put to death (31:32). Rachel escaped discovery by sitting on the gods while Laban searched her tent, but

Jewish scholars believe that Jacob had unwittingly placed her under a curse of death. They point out that she died during the birth of her next child and was buried by the wayside (35:16-20).[4] She was the only matriarch who was not buried in the cave of Machpelah.

The tense encounter between Jacob and Laban finally ended peaceably, and they concluded a treaty of nonaggression before going their separate ways. A heap of stones was set up as a witness to the treaty, which seems to have been a common practice in the ancient Near East (31:43-50). Early on the following day Jacob took his leave of Laban and set out to confront another rival, coming to meet him from the south (31:55–32:11).

Jacob and Esau

Jacob's route took him across the land of Gilead, which lay east of the Jordan River, and south toward Edom, where his brother Esau had settled. Remembering that Esau had vowed to kill him as soon as their father had died, Jacob sent an advance party with gifts to try to curry his brother's favor (32:3-5). The messengers soon returned with an alarming report. Esau was on his way to intercept Jacob, and four hundred warriors were at his side (32:6).

Jacob's situation was desperate. Never before had he encountered a problem that he felt incapable of handling. But this time things were different. It would have been too dangerous to try to return to Haran. He had run out of hiding places and had no choice except to face the wrath of an offended brother. An ancient Jewish proverb states that when a person has a clear conscience, everyone fears him, but when he has a guilty conscience, he fears everyone else.

Nightfall found him on the north bank of the Jabbok River near where it emptied into the Jordan, about midway between the Sea of Galilee and the Dead Sea. He had sent his family and flocks across, but he had tarried behind. The stage was set for one of the most dramatic experiences in Jacob's life. Verse 24 states that a mysterious night visitor, simply described as "a man" (32:24-25), wrestled with Jacob until the break of day. They were so evenly matched that it seemed as if their bout would end in a draw. However, Jacob was finally disabled by a blow that permanently dislocated his hip (32:25). In spite of his injury, he refused to let go of his opponent until he had been blessed. The blessing came in a change of names, from Jacob ("trickster" or "deceiver") to Israel ("may God rule"). The new name implied that Jacob was finally willing to let the reins of his life fall into the hands of God.

The night of wrestling left its mark on Jacob. He emerged from the ordeal a wounded and broken man. But his moment of failure was also his moment of triumph. God gave him a crippled body but a transformed faith. When dawn came and Jacob hobbled off to meet Esau, even Esau sensed that a change had come over his brother and ran to kiss him. He saw Jacob not as a man to be put to the sword but as a brother to be loved. Proverbs 16:7 reminds us: "When the ways of people please the Lord, he causes even their enemies to be at peace with them."

The overall impression we get of Jacob is that of a man who was always running from someone or something—either Esau, or Laban, or the famine in Canaan. Near the end of his life he made a poignant confession to Pharaoh: "Few and hard have been the years of my life" (47:9b). It is well for us to remember that Jacob was "Israel," and in the retelling of the stories of Jacob later Israelites saw in them a preview of their own checkered history of rebellion and flight. They should have learned from this ancestor that the way of victory is the way of surrender. One must be conquered by God in order to be ruled by God, and one must be ruled by God in order to be blessed by God.

Joseph and His Brothers

When [the LORD] summoned famine against the land, and broke every staff of bread, he had sent a man ahead of them, Joseph, who was sold as a slave. His feet were hurt with fetters. His neck was put in a collar of iron. Until what he had said came to pass, the word of the LORD kept testing him. The king sent and released him; the ruler of the people set him free. He made him lord of his house, and ruler of all his possessions, to instruct his officials at his pleasure, and to teach his elders wisdom. (Ps 105:16-22)

Because of its tightly-knit plot and its sharp delineation of characters, the story of Joseph has often been compared to a modern novel. It makes effective use of a device known as "dramatic reversal." It shows how God thwarts the will of evil persons by making their evil serve a good purpose. For example, Joseph was sold by his brothers so that they might be rid of his dreams, and yet his dreams came true. Joseph entered Egypt as a slave, and yet he rose to become a master. Joseph's brothers hated him, but through their hatred they brought suffering upon themselves. Joseph was cast out by his brothers, but his banishment enabled him to save them from starving. The abiding lesson in this story is that human evil cannot defeat the overriding purposes of divine grace.

The First Wise Man

Joseph personified the qualities of character that are praised in the book of Proverbs and other wisdom literature of ancient Israel. He was the prototype of the wise man of the Hebrew Scriptures. One of my seminary professors listed four indicators of Joseph's emotional and spiritual maturity: (1) a proper sense of balance between dependence and independence, (2) the ability to work with those whose philosophy of life was fundamentally different from his own, (3) the capacity to meet defeat with a minimum of conflict and without losing sight of his ultimate goal in life, and (4) a resolute determination to serve others and a refusal to lead a selfish life. Joseph's life serves as a worthy pattern for all who would live soberly, righteously, and godly in this present world.

A Story in Three Parts

The story of Joseph tells of one who was born to be a leader, but whose rise to leadership exposed him to jealousy, enslavement, temptation, false accusation, and imprisonment. And yet, through it all, God was guiding him to a higher destiny. His experience teaches us that God sometimes closes one door in order to open another. For example, there was only limited opportunity available in Potiphar's household. But the road from that limited opportunity to the larger opportunity in Pharaoh's court lay through a prison. The story of how Joseph traveled that road is told in three parts.

Part One. This part of the story has its setting in the household of Jacob in the land of Canaan (Gen 37). When the story opens, Jacob's sons are no longer children but grown men, although their behavior could still be described as childish. It is essentially a story of sibling rivalry, aided and abetted by the favoritism that Jacob showed toward Joseph, "the son of his old age" (37:3). Jacob had learned nothing from his own childhood when the favoritism of his parents drove a wedge between him and his brother Esau. Joseph aggravated the situation by playing the role of the spoiled brat and generally making himself obnoxious. As a lad of seventeen, he tattled on his older brothers (37:2), paraded before them in his fancy coat (37:3-4), and recounted to them his dreams of self-importance (37:5-11). At this stage in his life, no one could have predicted that he would someday be considered a model of wise thinking and mature judgment.

The two motifs introduced in chapter 37, the garment motif and the dream motif, continue to appear throughout the Joseph story. Joseph's coat initially served as a sign of his favored status, but when his brothers stripped it from him, dipped it in the blood of a slain goat,

and took it back to their father, it served as convincing evidence that
Joseph was dead. Whereupon, Jacob tore his garments, put on garments of sackcloth, and mourned many days for Joseph. (37:34).

The motif reappears in Egypt when Potiphar's wife grabs Joseph's
robe as he flees from her and uses it as evidence to falsely accuse
Joseph before her husband (39:11-18). A few years later, when Joseph
was summoned from prison to interpret Pharaoh's dream, he shaved
himself and put on fresh garments (41:14) in preparation for this royal
appointment. Pharaoh, on his part, was so impressed by Joseph's
wisdom and insight that he arrayed him in garments of fine linen and
appointed him to be second in command over the land of Egypt (41:42-
43). The final use of the garment motif occurs when Joseph is dis-
patching his brothers to Canaan to fetch their aged father. During the
parting festivities he presented a festal garment to each of the brothers,
except Benjamin, who received five garments (45:22). Joseph must
have done this to remind his brothers of how they had stripped him of
his garment before selling him into slavery. It may have been his way
of saying, "I forgive you."

The dream motif is also crucial to the plot of the Joseph story.
There are six dreams in all, two for Joseph (37:5, 9), two for Pharaoh's
officers in prison (40:5), and two for Pharaoh himself (41:1-7). The
Bible has surprisingly little to say about the interpreting of dreams. It is
instructive in this connection to compare Genesis 41 with Daniel 2.
Joseph and Daniel had quite similar experiences related to the interpretation of dreams. Each was exiled from his native land at an early
age. Each lived under a foreign ruler who had a disturbing dream that
his own wise men were incapable of interpreting. Each was summoned
to interpret the ruler's dream, and each was promoted to a position of
great honor and responsibility as a result of his giftedness (Gen 41: 39-
43; Dan 2:46-48). Finally, each of these young men attributed his
insights into the meaning of dreams to God alone (Gen 41:16; Dan
2:27-28).

Part Two. The second part of the Joseph story describes Joseph's
early years in Egypt and his rise "from rags to riches" (Gen 39–41).
His climb to the top began when he was made overseer of Potiphar's
household and charged with the management of all he owned. The
theme of blessing reappears at this point in the story, for we are told
that from the time Joseph assumed his duties, "The LORD blessed the
Egyptian's house for Joseph's sake; the blessing of the LORD was on
all that he had, in house and field" (39:5).

Joseph's new position and his handsome appearance (39:6b)
exposed him to a new threat. Potiphar's wife was infatuated with him
and attempted to seduce him when they were alone in the house. Since

he was but a lowly slave and she was the mistress of the house, she obviously expected him to give in to her advances. She attempted to seduce him not once but many times (39:10). Joseph was in a very awkward position. He had to face the woman's advances so long as he kept his job. He could not ask to be transferred to another job without arousing Potiphar's suspicions and the woman's ire. All he could do was to seek to dissuade the woman and avoid her presence (39:8-10).

But Potiphar's wife was not the kind of person who would take no for an answer. Since flattery and persuasion had failed, she resorted to force. When she and Joseph were alone in the house, she took hold of his coat and refused to let go. Joseph's only recourse was to flee from the scene without his coat, although the coat could later be used as incriminating evidence against him. The decision to run was not the action of a coward but of a brave man, for it cost him both his job and his freedom.

And what was his reward for this signal act of bravery? He was allowed to be thrown into prison, where he had to mark time for a matter of years. Surely God could have handled the situation better than this! Why did God not send an earthquake to destroy the prison and set the faithful servant free? Claus Westermann poses this same question and comes up with the following answer.

> The narrator intends to say through this that God really is like this. [God] does not allow [God's] deeds to be calculated . . . , even by [God's] own [servants]. [God] is not the dear God of pious history where everything always goes right. . . . It is possible that a decision made in obedience to God can bring a [person] directly into catastrophe. There is no question of an appeal.[5]

We know the truth of this statement when we remember the experiences of individuals such as Jeremiah, John the Baptist, John Bunyan, and Dietrich Bonhoeffer (see Heb 11:35-38).

Joseph had the rare ability to turn liabilities into assets. His term in prison might have broken a weaker person, but for him it was only a momentary detour in his pilgrimage of faith. The secret of his endurance was God's presence in his life (39:21-23). During the lengthy stay behind bars he might have been tempted to doubt the reality of God's presence and power, but there is no indication that he ever did. His life was so completely surrendered to God that he could afford to wait for God to make the next move.

Opportunity came knocking at the prison door when Pharaoh dreamed his difficult dreams and summoned Joseph to interpret them. Joseph helped Pharaoh to foresee the coming years of famine and to make preparation for them. It has been said that the reward for a task well done is a larger task. Joseph had served well in Potiphar's household as well as in prison. Because of his excellent advice about the famine, Pharaoh elevated him to a position of authority over all the land of Egypt, second only to Pharaoh. Joseph had emerged triumphant from the test of adversity. And the famine in Egypt had set the stage for a reunion between himself and his brothers.

Part Three. The conditions that produced the famine in Egypt also affected the land of Canaan. Jacob and his remaining sons eventually felt the effects and had to take some action. Upon hearing that there was grain in Egypt, Jacob sent all of his sons except Benjamin to purchase food for the family. Benjamin was kept at home because Jacob feared losing him as he had earlier lost Joseph (42:1-5).

When the brothers arrived, Joseph immediately recognized them, although they did not know him. He allowed them to buy grain but put them through a series of tests before permitting them to return home. For three days they were held in prison on the charge that they were spies. They staunchly denied the charge. Joseph then released all of them except Simeon and sent them back to Canaan. He told them not to return unless they brought their youngest brother Benjamin as evidence that they were telling the truth.

The famine in Canaan did not let up, and it eventually mandated a second trip to Egypt. At first, Jacob refused to permit Benjamin to accompany his brothers but was forced to relent by the severity of the famine. Joseph's strategy in demanding that Benjamin be brought to Egypt was to pose one final test for his brothers. He wanted to see if there had been any change in their character since the Shechem days. He first laid a trap for them by making it appear that Benjamin had stolen his silver divining cup (44:1-13). He then offered to punish only Benjamin by holding him in prison and permitting the rest of the brothers to return to Canaan. Joseph's purpose was to see if the brothers would stand with Benjamin or abandon him to his fate, as they had once abandoned Joseph himself.

The answer was not long in coming. Judah quickly stepped forward to make an impassioned plea for his younger brother. He even offered to take Benjamin's place in prison and pay his penalty so that their father might not be freshly grieved. Joseph was so moved by this demonstration of brotherly love and loyalty that he could no longer restrain himself. He made himself known to his brothers and celebrated with them the recovery of their lost unity. He then dispatched them to Canaan to fetch their father and their families. With Jacob's arrival in Egypt, the stage was set for the events leading up to the enslavement of his descendants and their eventual exodus out of Egypt.

Judah

The study of Genesis would not be complete without some attention being given to Judah and to the role he and his descendants were destined to play in Israelite history. In the Joseph story Judah often functions as the spokesman for his brothers (see Gen 37:26; 43:3, 8; 44:14, 16, 18; 46:28). He also plays a prominent role in the story of Tamar, inserted between chapters 37 and 39 of Genesis. Finally, Jacob virtually passes the patriarchal torch to Judah when he delivers to him the blessing recorded in Genesis 49:8-12.

Judah and His Brothers

The exact part Judah played in the sale of Joseph is left unclear and has been variously interpreted. He prevented his brothers from killing Joseph by offering an alternative plan: "What profit is it if we kill our brother and conceal his blood? Come, let us sell him to the Ishmaelites, and not lay our hands on him, for he is our brother, our own flesh" (37:26-27). At first sight this seems like a noble effort on Judah's part to foil the plot to have Joseph put to death. Other commentators, however, see nothing but crass materialism in his suggestion that Joseph be sold to traders. They point out that the word translated "profit" has mercenary overtones similar to our words for "loot" or "rake-off." These interpreters believe that Judah was motivated solely by self-interest.

The next time Judah played a prominent part in the Joseph story was when he and his brothers were organizing a second expedition to Egypt to buy bread. They had been warned not to come again unless Benjamin accompanied them. Jacob held up the return as long as he could, unwilling to risk the loss of Benjamin, the last of Rachel's two sons. In his frustration he cried out, "Why have you treated me so badly? Why did you tell the man that you had yet another brother?" (43:6, NEB). Judah then tried to break the deadlock by offering to become surety for Benjamin and vowing to bring him back safely or else forfeit his own life (43:8-10). Jacob finally gave in to Judah's appeal, resigning himself to his fate by saying, "If I am bereaved of my children, I am bereaved" (43:14b).

What happened after the brothers arrived in Egypt has already been noted. Our concern here is with the role that Judah played in these events. When Benjamin had been implicated in the theft of Joseph's divining cup, it was Judah who offered himself as a ransom for his younger brother. He who had at first suggested selling Joseph into slavery was now willing to become a slave himself in order that Benjamin might be set free to return to his father. This was dramatic proof of Judah's moral and spiritual growth.

Judah and Tamar

The story of Judah and Tamar is sandwiched between chapters 37 and 39 of Genesis, both of which deal with the beginning of Joseph's career. Nevertheless, there are significant links between chapter 38 and its context. First, both chapter 37 and chapter 38 focus attention on important episodes in the life of Judah. The first chapter records Judah's successful attempt to spare the life of Joseph (37:26-27); the second tells how Judah unwittingly fathered twins by his daughter-in-law Tamar (38:1ff.). Again, chapters 38 and 39 are linked by their subject matter. Each deals with the efforts of a woman to attract the attention of a man. Tamar was an honorable woman seeking to safeguard the interests of her deceased husband, even if it involved risking her life. Potiphar's wife, on the other hand, was an adulterous woman who had no concern for the interests of her husband or for Joseph. A further link between chapters 38 and 39 is their use of the garment motif. Chapter 38 recounts how Tamar, desiring to become pregnant by her father-in-law Judah, changed from her widow's garment to those of a harlot in order to seduce Judah as he passed her way. Chapter 39 tells how Potiphar's wife seized Joseph's coat and falsely accused him of trying to seduce her. Finally, the birth of the twins, Perez and Zerah (38:27-30), is linked to Jacob's blessing of Judah (49:8-12). Through Perez, the older of the twins, Tamar and Judah became ancestors of David, founder of the kingdom of Judah, and the inspiration behind the messianic hope of the Hebrew Scriptures (see Ruth 4:12; 1 Chron 2:4; Matt 1:3).

Tamar, of course, was an unlikely ancestress of the Messiah since she was a Canaanite (38:1-6), a daughter of the very people whom Abraham considered unfit to intermarry with a Hebrew (24:2-4). Because of Tamar's concern to bear children for the sake of her deceased husband, Judah was forced to confess, "She is in the right than I, since I did not give her to my son Shelah" (38:26).

Judah and Jacob

As Jacob's life drew to a close, a major decision had to be made. Who among his twelve sons would be chosen as the recipient of the birthright and the bearer of the patriarchal blessing? The three leading candidates for this honor were Reuben (Jacob's firstborn), Joseph (Rachel's first son), and Judah. Reuben effectively removed himself from consideration when he lay with Bilhah, Jacob's concubine, and fell into disfavor (Gen 35:22; 49:3-4; 1 Chron 5:1).

Joseph seems to have had an early lead over the others. His dreams indicated that his brothers would bow down to him (37:5-11), and the dreams were fulfilled (42:6; 43:26-28). Furthermore, Jacob pronounced a special blessing on Joseph and Joseph's two sons, Ephraim and Manasseh (48:15-22; 49:22-26; see also Deut 33:13-17; 1 Chron 5:1-2).

There can be no doubt that Joseph and the two Joseph tribes of Ephraim and Manasseh were early favorites for the right to inherit the patriarchal blessing. But this was not the way it turned out in the end. As Psalm 78 informs us, the descendants of Ephraim forfeited their right to rule (vv. 9-11), the house of Joseph was rejected (v. 67), and God's choice ultimately fell on Judah and the house of David (vv. 68-72).

This probably accounts for the wording of Jacob's blessing to Judah in Genesis 49. The main thrust of the blessing lies in verses 8 and 10:

> Judah, your brothers shall praise you; your hand shall be on the neck of your enemies; your father's sons shall bow down before you. . . .
> The scepter shall not depart from Judah, nor the ruler's staff from between his feet, until tribute comes to him; and the obedience of the peoples is his.

Comparing this promise with the many not-so-subtle signs of Judah's rise to prominence in the book of Genesis leads to one conclusion. The promise of dominion, first delivered to Jacob (27:27-29), is ultimately transferred to Judah. One Jewish writer commented on Jacob's blessing of Judah in these words:

> Joseph has always had the deep affection of his father, whose favorable words . . . form a fitting summary of the life of his great son. The ultimate focus, however, is on Judah. It is through him that God's mysterious designs will be carried on. When the poem turns to Judah, it turns resolutely to the future . . . and, in light of history, the prophecy turned out to be remarkably accurate. It was Judah's tribe that survived destruction and deportation by the Babylonians (586 B.C.E.) and that provided continuity for the children of Israel.[6]

Christians would want to take this a step further. The one to whom all authority in heaven and on earth has been given is Jesus Christ. He was born of the line of David and is a true descendant of the tribe of Judah (see Matt 1:1-3). Jacob's blessing was right on target.

Conclusion

We have come to the end of Genesis, where we find ourselves standing between the giving of the patriarchal promises and their fulfillment. Genesis opens with the words "in the beginning God" and closes with the phrase "in a coffin in Egypt." It would have been catastrophic if this had indeed been the end of the story, if there had been no Exodus, no Sinai, no promised land, no Messiah from the tribe of Judah!

But God, who had always been a faithful promise-keeper, did not abandon the descendants of Abraham. The patriarchs all died without receiving the promises, but their faith taught them that God who had begun a work in them would bring it to completion in their children. Their call and election were but the beginning of God's mighty acts on their behalf.

Notes

[1]W. Gunther Plaut, "Genesis," in *The Torah: A Modern Commentary* (New York: Union of American Hebrew Congregations, 1974) 261.

[2]See, e.g., ibid., 283.

[3]Robert Alter, *The Art of Biblical Narrative* (New York: Basic Books, 1981) 52.

[4]Plaut, 312.

[5]Claus Westermann, *A Thousand Years and a Day*, trans. Stanley Rudman (Philadelphia: Fortress Press, 1962) 49.

[6]Plaut, 472.

Chapter 4

Out of Egypt

Exodus 1:1–15:21

Few events have so profoundly affected the course of history as Israel's exodus out of Egypt. Hebrew slaves were toiling to build storage cities for Pharaohs Sethos I (1309-1290 B.C.) and his son and successor, Ramses II (1290-1224 B.C.), when God called Moses to lead them to freedom. After considerable delay and endless haggling with Pharaoh, Moses was finally able to secure the liberation of the Hebrews. The night of their departure from Egypt was marked by the inauguration of the Passover, a festival of freedom that has continued to be celebrated for more than three thousand years.

The Exodus played a major role in the development of Israel's self-understanding. For one thing, it taught Israel that God's promises were still valid even after centuries of postponed fulfillment. It had been more than four hundred years since Jacob and his family had migrated to Egypt (Exod 12:40). In the meantime, their descendants had been enslaved and subjected to cruelty and injustice. Still this did not mean that God had abandoned them. This is made clear by the way in which God first spoke to Moses at the burning bush when God said,

> I am the God of your fathers, the God of Abraham, the God of Isaac, and the God of Jacob. . . . I have observed the misery of my people . . . , I have heard their cry . . . I know their sufferings, and I have come down to deliver them from the Egyptians. (Exod 3:6-8a)

God's enduring memory gave hope to the oppressed Hebrew people.

The Exodus experience also taught Israel the meaning of its election to be the recipient of God's special revelation. According to the Talmud, God's revelation was first offered to the great nations of the earth, but when they heard its contents, they refused it. God then offered it to the enslaved people of Israel, and they agreed to accept it. This legendary story shows that at least some of the Israelites understood their election not so much as the bestowal of special privilege but as the acceptance of special responsibility. Israel's election actually exposed that nation to greater trials and hardships than other nations had to face.

It was through the Exodus also that Israel came to value human freedom. Once the Hebrews were freed from Egyptian bondage, they were never again content to be slaves to anyone. From then on, they valued their freedom as a gift from God. Even when they suffered temporary enslavement, as happened so often throughout their troubled history, the ideal of freedom never died. The generations that followed Moses learned to pray, "This year Jews are enslaved; may next year set them free."[1] Also because of the Exodus experience, the remainder of the Hebrew Scriptures exhibits a deep-seated bias in favor of the world's weak, downtrodden, and oppressed peoples. God came to be portrayed as the champion and friend of the unprotected members of society such as foreigners, widows, orphans, and slaves. The Bible is always suspicious of those who grow powerful and wealthy while most of their neighbors remain poor and weak. The Exodus experience furnished the foundation for the ethical preaching of the great prophets with their demand for justice and righteousness in human affairs (see Isa 1:12-17; 5:7; Amos 5:21-24).

The Exodus experience led to a rebirth of faith and hope among the dispirited Hebrews. Their long sojourn in Egypt, climaxed by their years of servitude, had caused their faith to wear thin. When it is reported that they groaned under their bondage and cried out for help, the writer avoids saying that they cried out to God (Exod 2:23). Perhaps their bitter suffering had caused them to forget God and God's promises to their ancestors. If the Exodus had not occurred, it is entirely possible that their faith would have disappeared altogether. But the Exodus did occur, and their faltering faith received new life. The book of Exodus pinpoints the precise moment when their faith was reborn.

> Thus the Lord saved Israel that day from the hand of the Egyptians; and Israel saw the Egyptians dead upon the seashore. Israel saw the great work that the Lord did against the Egyptians. So the people feared the Lord and believed in the Lord and in his servant Moses. (Exod 14:30-31)

The story of the Exodus is not one that a nation would have invented about itself. God chose a weak, dispirited people whom the world treated as outcasts. In the midst of their oppression, there was no protecting law to which they might appeal. God had chosen them not because of who they were, but because of who God was, a God of grace and forgiveness, whose ear was open to the cry of the needy. Pagan gods would have chosen the strong and the wealthy to bear their name. These could have repaid them with magnificent temples and generous sacrifices. But God chose a group of nobodies, a people without power, wealth, or credentials to bear God's name and to bless the world. Truly God's ways are past finding out.

Oppression in Egypt
1:1-22

The opening verses of Exodus recap the story of how Jacob and seventy members of his family joined Joseph in Egypt and how they eventually multiplied and grew "exceedingly strong" (1:1-8). Then after many years there arose a pharaoh who did not know of the worthwhile achievements of Joseph (1:8). Fearful of the growing numbers of the Hebrews, this ruling pharaoh enslaved them and put them to work building the royal storage cities of Pithom and Ramses (1:11) in the hope that hard work might slow their rate of growth. But the principle of "dramatic reversal" again came into play, and the more the Hebrews were oppressed, the more they multiplied (1:12).

Having failed in his initial attempt to suppress the Hebrews, Pharaoh devised a harsher plan. He summoned Shiphrah and Puah, midwives who attended the Hebrew women in childbirth, and instructed them to put to death all the male children born to the Hebrews. But because the midwives "feared God," they ignored Pharaoh's instructions and let the male children live (1:17). Their explanation to Pharaoh was that Hebrew women were so vigorous, they gave birth to their children without the help of midwives (1:19). Not to be outdone, Pharaoh handed down a decree that every male child born to the Hebrews henceforth should be thrown into the Nile (1:22). This diabolical command set the stage for the birth of Moses and his timely rescue from the waters of the Nile.

Moses' Birth and Early Manhood
2:1-15a

Another example of "dramatic reversal" can be seen in the role women played in the unfolding drama of the Exodus. Pharaoh was so obsessed by what he perceived to be the threat from Hebrew males that he failed to take note of an even greater threat from the females of his kingdom, including his own daughter. The involvement of women began with the fertility of the Hebrew women and the courageous stance of the two midwives. Then Moses' mother and sister were teamed up with Pharaoh's daughter to further outwit the ruler. Later, when Moses fled from Egypt, he was greeted by women at a well in the land of Midian. One of these women, Zipporah, became Moses' wife and later saved his life as they were on their way back to Egypt (4:24-26). The last scene in the Exodus drama features a choir of women led by Miriam, employing music, dance, and song in the celebration of Pharaoh's downfall (15:20-21). In every respect, Pharaoh had more to fear from women than from men. In recognition of this, the Jewish Talmud concluded that Israel was redeemed from bondage because of its righteous women.[2]

Moses as a Baby (2:1-10)

God often performs miracles through fragile and insignificant means. A slave shack in Egypt became the birthplace of Moses, Aaron, and Miriam, all of whom were destined to play a leading role in the liberation of their people. Moses was born under a death threat and barely managed to survive. For a while the future of God's plan of the ages rested with this helpless infant set adrift on the crocodile-infested waters of the Nile in a homemade wicker basket. Only God can afford to take risks like that.

The word used to designate Moses' ark is *tebah*, which is used in the Bible only here and in the Genesis account of Noah's ark. Thus both Moses and Noah were saved from drowning by a *tebah*, an ark. And each of these was spared so that others might enjoy freedom and new life.

Moses as a Young Man (2:11-15a)

There is a time lapse of almost forty years between verses 10 and 11 of the second chapter of Exodus (see Acts 7:23). In verse 10 Moses is a newly-weaned baby, whereas in the following verse he is a grown man. We are left in the dark about what might have occurred during the intervening years, although the Jewish Talmud uses legendary materials to fill in some of the gaps. There is a parallel between the silent years in the life of Moses and the similar period in the life of Jesus.

One day after Moses was grown, he decided to visit the workplace of the Hebrew slaves (Exod 2:11). While there, he witnessed the killing of a Hebrew slave by one of the Egyptian taskmasters. Moses' anger flared at the sight of this crime, and he leaped upon the offender and killed him, supposing that no one had seen what he had done. On the following day, however, Moses returned to the scene and found one of the Hebrew slaves trying to kill a fellow slave. Moses tried to negotiate a settlement of their dispute only to have them turn on him and threaten to reveal his secret. In the sermon Stephen preached prior to being stoned to death, he drew upon this experience of Moses to develop the theme of the rejected deliverer as it applied to Christ (Acts 7:23-29).

This episode in the life of Moses reveals a number of traits that keep reappearing throughout his career. These characteristics include his readiness to be identified with the Hebrew slaves, his anger at the sight of wrong, his readiness to intervene on the side of the victims of wrong, his willingness to assume the role of a mediator, and his tendency to overreact.

Moses' killing of the Egyptian certainly was a high-handed act, undertaken without God's command or permission. Furthermore, there was no word of commendation or reassurance from God after the incident. Once Moses' deed was known, he felt forced to flee like a common criminal and seek asylum in the desert. After this false start Moses spent forty more years of his life in the desert before God sent him back to Egypt (Exod 7:7; see Acts 7:30-34).

Moses in Midian

2:15–4:26

Moses found refuge near Sinai among bedouin tribesmen known as Midianites. According to Genesis 25:1-2, Midian was the son of Abraham by his wife Keturah. Midianite traders are reported to have taken Joseph to be sold into Egypt (Gen 37:28).

As Moses rested beside a well in the land of Midian, seven daughters of Jethro, the priest of Midian, came to water their father's flock. As soon as the women filled the watering troughs, other shepherds tried to drive them away and take the water for their own flocks. But once again it was Moses who came to the rescue. His sense of justice would not let him remain silent while others were being mistreated. Perhaps most of his contemporaries thought of women as having no rights, but Moses did not share such a view.

When the women returned home, their father asked how they had managed to arrive so early in the day. They replied that an Egyptian had come to their rescue and had helped to water their flock (2:19). The father then scolded them for not having invited the friendly stranger to accept food and lodging in their home. Their oversight was soon corrected, and Moses was invited to come home with them. He accepted their invitation and stayed forty years! His own people had rejected him, but in the tent of a Midianite he found true hospitality. He also found a wife among Jethro's daughters, and she later bore him a son named Gershom.

The pharaoh who began the persecution of the Hebrews, Sethos I, died in 1290 B.C. and was succeeded by his son Ramses II (1290–1224

B.C.). The persecution of the Hebrews continued unabated under
Ramses. The Hebrews then cried out for help, and their cry came up
to God (2:23-25). God was ready to bring their bondage to an end and
chose to do this through Moses who was uniquely qualified for the
task. Moses had not only been reared in Pharaoh's court, but he had
also been schooled in the rigors of desert living for forty years. He was
providentially prepared to lead the Hebrews through this same barren
wasteland. This does not mean, of course, that Moses was ready to
volunteer for the mission.

The Call of Moses

Moses' call to return to Egypt resembles other call accounts found in
the Bible, including those of Abraham (Gen 12:1-3), Gideon (Jgs 6:11-
40), Saul (1 Sam 9:1–10:13), Isaiah (Isa 6:1-8), Jeremiah (Jer 1:4-10),
Ezekiel (Ezek 1:1–3:15), and Paul (Acts 9:1-19). We will note five
central features that most of these calls shared.

The first involves the vision that normally accompanies a person's
call to special service for God. Isaiah saw the Lord sitting upon a
throne and surrounded by choirs of seraphim. Ezekiel saw a chariot-
throne carried through the air by indescribably strange creatures.
Moses saw a bush that burned without being consumed. Paul saw a
blinding light at midday.

The second feature was the voice of command that described the
mission and called for commitment. The climax of the call came not in
what was seen but in what was heard. Abraham was asked to separate
himself from his country and kindred in order to become a blessing to
all nations. Isaiah was told to go and preach to a people who had their
ears and eyes sealed against the truth. Jeremiah heard that God had
consecrated him from birth to be a prophet to the nations. Moses was
told to return to Egypt and to command Pharaoh in the Lord's name
to let the Hebrews go free.

A third feature involves the wide range of responses made to the
call of God. These fall into two broad categories, consisting of the
"volunteers" and the "draft-dodgers." Persons such as Abraham,
Isaiah, and Ezekiel accepted God's call with submission, if not
outright enthusiasm. The "draft-dodgers" included Moses, Gideon,
Saul, and Jeremiah. Those in this latter group tried to persuade God
that it was a mistake to call them. None protested as long or as loudly
as Moses.

A fourth feature woven into many of the call accounts is the fore-
warning of rejection. God never minimized the cost of discipleship in
order to pad the roll of disciples. One committed disciple was worth

more than a whole company of halfhearted followers. Jesus urged those who would follow him to count the cost at the beginning in order to avoid faltering in mid-course (Luke 14:25-33). Moses was warned in advance that Pharaoh would harden his heart and refuse to let the Hebrews go until he had been thoroughly subdued (Exod 4:21).

The fifth element in these call narratives is the promise of God's continuing presence for the duration of the mission. To the protesting Moses came this assurance: "I will be with you; and this [God's presence] shall be the sign for you that it is I who sent you" (3:12a). Jeremiah was told: "Do not be afraid of them, for I am with you to deliver you, says the Lord" (Jer 1:8). Jesus promised all who would serve him, "I am with you always, to the end of the age" (Matt 28:20). Such a promise is more valuable than all of earth's success symbols.

News travels fast in the desert, and Moses probably heard from passing caravans that the pharaoh who had once sought his life was now dead (see Exod 2:23). Still, he was not ready to return to the aid of his people. When God called him to undertake such a mission, he offered excuse after excuse for refusing to obey. He claimed his unworthiness: "Who am I that I should go to Pharaoh, and bring the Israelites out of Egypt?" (3:11). He protested that if the Israelites asked to know the name of the God who had sent him, he would not know how to respond (3:13). He complained that the Israelites simply would not believe that the Lord had sent him (4:1). He pleaded his inability to speak (4:10). Finally, he tried to withdraw his name by asking the Lord to send someone else (4:13). This angered the Lord, and Moses was ordered to obey without further ado (4:14-17).

Some attention needs to be given to the revelation of God's name to Moses (3:15-18; see 6:2-3). God's response when Moses asked, "What is his name?" (2:13), was both an answer and the refusal of an answer. God simply said, "I AM WHO I AM" (3:14), an enigmatic reply based on the verb *hayah*, "to be," and translatable in the future as well as in the present tense. Thus, many have taken it to mean "I will be what I will be," that is, "I will be whatever tomorrow demands." God is further identified to Moses as YHWH, translated "LORD" (always capitalized in English translations). In 6:2-3, God says, "I am *YHWH*. I appeared to Abraham, Isaac, and Jacob as *El Shaddai* (God Almighty), but by my name '*YHWH*,' I did not make myself known to them." Many believe that this new covenant name for God also is based upon the verb "to be" (*hayah*). Thus, Moffatt's translation renders YHWH as "the Eternal," that is, "the One who is." Others prefer a causative sense, enabling it to be read as "the One who causes to be," that is, "the Creator God." Whatever the derivation of this untranslatable name, it is used throughout the Hebrew

Scriptures of One who is steadfast in purpose to save and adequate for every situation one may face. With such a God at his side, Moses could be assured of the success of his mission (3:11-12).

The Contest Between God and Pharaoh

7–11

God sent a series of ten plagues to soften Pharaoh's resistance to the departure of the Hebrews and to show who was really in charge of matters in Egypt. The scene is described by Fretheim as "a picture of creation gone berserk."[3] Bizarre things began to happen in this land where life was normally quite predictable and dependable. J. Edgar Parks describes the gradual worsening of the situation in these words.

> One can read the list of plagues like a tragic history of the troubles of life. Starting with general unpleasantness, like the lack of good water and the stink of dead fish; followed by unpleasant company, hopping and croaking around everywhere; then stinging flocks of minor irritations, lice and flies; till in full earnest comes real sickness of man and beast, boils and blains and murrain; followed by storms, lightning, and hail; and real enemies in battalions, locusts, the first inventors of the scorched earth policy; then terror of darkness; and [after that] death.[4]

The Hardening of Pharaoh's Heart

How are we to determine who was responsible for Pharaoh's stubborn refusal to let the Hebrews go free? On the one hand, we are told that it was God who hardened Pharaoh's heart (see 7:3; 9:12; 10:1, 20, 27; 11:10). Other passages report that Pharaoh hardened his own heart (see 8:15, 32; 9:34).

The author of the book of Exodus makes no attempt to harmonize these two viewpoints. What we have here is an illustration of the paradox of human freedom and divine sovereignty. Wwhile Pharaoh was a free moral agent pursuing his own course of action and fully responsible for his own misdeeds, God still maintained ultimate control over the situation. It was God and not Pharaoh who would determine the outcome. Pharaoh was given plenty of rope, but the end of the rope was still held firmly in the hand of God. Paul understood God's reason for putting up with Pharaoh's stubbornness when he wrote these words: "The scripture says to Pharaoh, 'I have raised you up for the very purpose of showing my power in you, so that my name may be proclaimed in all the earth' " (Rom 9:17).

The story of the wearing down of Pharaoh's resistance is told as if it were a complicated piece of oriental bargaining. In the beginning Pharaoh's magicians were able to duplicate the changing of Aaron's rod into a serpent (7:10-13), the changing of water into blood (7:22), and the multiplication of the frogs (8:7). After the third plague, Pharaoh proposed a slight compromise by offering to let the Hebrews offer sacrifices to their God in the land of Egypt (8:25), a plan Moses flatly rejected. Pharaoh then proposed that the Israelites go only a short distance outside the land of Egypt to offer their sacrifices (8:28). After the seventh plague, Pharaoh confessed that he had sinned and offered to let the Hebrews go, only to harden his heart immediately afterwards (9:27-28, 34). He then tried to negotiate another compromise with Moses; he would agree to let the men go if they would leave their wives and children behind (10:8-11). Moses again refused the compromise. After the plague of darkness, Pharaoh made a final attempt to effect a compromise. He offered to let the Hebrews depart if they would leave their flocks and herds behind (10:24). Again Moses refused to compromise, although it required the plague of death on all the firstborns of the land of Egypt to finally convince Pharaoh of the futility of further resistance.

The Despoiling of the Egyptians

At the time of Moses' call, the Lord said to him,

> I will bring this people into such favor with the Egyptians that, when you go [out of Egypt], you will not go empty-handed; each woman shall ask her neighbor and any woman living in the neighbor's house for jewelry of silver and of gold, and clothing, and you shall put them on your sons and on your daughters; and so you shall plunder the Egyptians. (3:21-22)

This command is repeated in 11:2, and the record of its fulfillment is found in 12:35-36. Exodus 11:3 seems to indicate that the Egyptians were willing to share with the departing Israelites because of the high esteem they held for Moses.

Some readers have questioned the ethics of Hebrew women who would ask for expensive gifts of jewelry and clothing when they had no intentions of returning these to their owners. Does not such behavior smack of deception? Most commentaries answer in the negative. The Hebrew Scriptures require that no freed slave should be sent away from a former owner empty-handed. Deuteronomy 15:12-14 best expresses this requirement:

> If a member of your community, whether a Hebrew man or a
> Hebrew woman, is sold to you and works for you six years, in the
> seventh year you shall set that person free. And when you send a
> male slave out from you a free person, you shall not send him out
> empty-handed. Provide liberally out of your flock, your threshing
> floor, and your wine press, thus giving to him some of the bounty
> with which the Lord your God has blessed you. Remember that you
> were a slave in the land of Egypt, and the Lord your God redeemed
> you; for this reason I lay this upon you today.

Clements sums up the situation in these words: "The spoiling of the
Egyptians was to serve as a punishment for the ill-treatment of the
Hebrew slaves, and also as a payment for the work they had been
forced to do. Thus, in the narrator's eyes, it was an act of divine
justice."[5]

Freedom at Last

12–15

The Bible reports that the Israelites left Egypt at midnight on the
fourteenth day of the month of Abib (later called Nisan), which corresponds to our March or April (see 12:18; 13:3-4). The full moon
always appears on the fourteenth day of the month in the Jewish
calendar. Therefore, the Israelites had additional light for their
journey. Since that memorable night some three thousand years ago,
the Passover has continued to be celebrated as a memorial to Israel's
march to freedom. The population of Israel had already greatly
increased, thus fulfilling the first part of God's promise to Abraham.
Their departure from Egypt meant that they were about to receive the
second part of the promise, namely, a homeland of their own.

Exodus 12:38 reports that "a mixed multitude" accompanied the
Hebrews as they left Egypt. This information led Fretheim to observe:

> They were a "mixed crowd," consisting of more than the descen-
> dants of the twelve sons of Jacob. Many non-Israelites had been
> integrated into the community of faith, and other communities no
> doubt took advantage of the opportunity to choose freedom. *Freedom
> for Israel means freedom for others* (see 22:21; 23:9). When the people
> of God are liberated, not only their own kind can come along. The
> benefits of freedom have a fallout effect on all those with whom they
> come in contact, whether they are people of faith or not. So it has
> been throughout the centuries, often in spite of efforts by the people
> of God to become a community unto themselves. God's redemption
> is not for the chosen few; it is for the sake of all of the world. Would

that every community where the people of God are gathered could be called a "mixed crowd."[6]

Victory at the Sea

According to Exodus 14:1-2, God commanded the Hebrews to turn back after their initial attempt to leave Egypt and to encamp at a place named Pi-ha-hiroth. Apparently they had been unable to get past Pharaoh's soldiers guarding the northern frontier of the country. Pharaoh interpreted their turning back as an indication that they were lost and sent his best-equipped troops to pursue them (14:3-9). The Hebrews suddenly found themselves trapped between Pharaoh's army and the waters of the Red Sea.

The Hebrews turned in despair to Moses and asked, "Was it because there were no graves in Egypt that you have taken us away to die in the wilderness?" (Exod 14:11a.) There was a note of bitter irony in their question, for everyone knew that Egypt was famous for its giant pyramid tombs. Moses responded by calling them to put their trust in God: "Do not be afraid, stand firm, and see the deliverance that the Lord will accomplish for you today; for the Egyptians whom you see today you shall never see again. The Lord will fight for you, and you have only to keep still" (14:13-14a).

The Hebrews did not understand that a way is usually provided for God's people *through* their difficulties, not *around* them. The same truth is meaningfully expressed in Isaiah 43:1-2:

> Thus says the Lord, he who created you, O Jacob, he who formed you, O Israel: "Do not fear, for I have redeemed you; I have called you by name, you are mine. When you pass through the waters, I will be with you; and through the rivers, they shall not overwhelm you; when you walk through fire you shall not be burned, and the flame shall not consume you."

The crossing of the sea highlights the relationship between the natural and the supernatural in the Hebrew Scriptures. For instance, Moses is told to stretch out his rod over the sea and cause the waters to divide (4:16). On the other hand, we are informed that a strong east wind blew all night and cleared a path through the sea (14:21). Childs speaks of this miracle as involving both the wonderful and the ordinary.

> The waters were split by the rod of Moses, but a strong wind blew all night and laid bare the sea bed. The waters stood up as a mighty wall to the left and the right, and yet the Egyptians were drowned when

the sea returned to its normal channels. Yahweh produced panic with his fiery glance, but it was the mud of the sea bottom which clogged the wheels of the heavy chariots. The elements of the wonderful and the ordinary are constitutive to the greatest of Old Testament events. There never was a time when the event was only understood as ordinary, nor was there a time when the supernatural absorbed the natural. But Israel saw the mighty hand of God at work in both the ordinary and the wonderful, and never sought to fragment the one great act of redemption into parts.[7]

Whatever the method employed, it was God who brought about the downfall of the Egyptians and rescued Israel from destruction. Plaut sums up the matter in these words: "[God] may have used wind and water, cloud and darkness as [God's] agents, but it was [God's] will that Israel be saved, and saved it was."[8]

The theologically significant word "to save" occurs in 14:30: "Thus the Lord saved Israel that day from the Egyptians." This is the first occurrence of this word in the Hebrew Scriptures with God as the subject. The basic meaning of the verb "to save" is "to be wide, spacious, free." Salvation means freedom–freedom from confinement, freedom to breathe, freedom to live. To the Hebrews it meant freedom from bondage and the sting of the oppressor's lash. Wherever people are victimized by injustice, oppression, poverty, ignorance, disease, or hunger, God is concerned that they be set free. God is no less concerned for their release from sin's bondage. Jesus emphasized this aspect of salvation when he said, "If the Son makes you free, you will be free indeed" (John 8:36). This is why Paul could speak of "the freedom of the glory of the children of God" (Rom 8:21).

A Faith that Sings

The prose account of the crossing of the sea (14:21-31) is followed by hymns of praise celebrating God's mighty power and tender care for Israel (15:1-21). The Exodus narrative thus begins with a cry of distress (2:23) and ends with a shout of praise. Rhodes notes the contrast between the beginning and the end of the story:

What a relief! A song, a paean of praise, after fourteen chapters of intense and dramatic action! This is poetry, folk poetry, the kind of poetry that sticks in one's memory and is sung around the campfire, or on the trail, or in a commemorative worship service. Yet it is poetry grounded in history; it brings to mind something that happened; it dramatizes an event.[9]

Israel's crossing of the sea and its safe passage through the wilderness speak to us of God's tender love and mighty power to deliver. This is fittingly summed up in 15:13: "In your steadfast love you led the people whom you redeemed; you guided them by your strength to your holy abode." Here God's steadfast love and strength are brought together as complementary terms.

All our basic questions about God could be reduced to two: "Is God able?" and "Does God care?" To believe in a God who was concerned about the human predicament but powerless to do anything about it still would leave us in despair. On the other hand, to believe in a God who was all-powerful and yet unconcerned about our predicament would leave us as though we were hopeless wanderers in a hostile universe. True hope is grounded in a recognition of God's power *and* God's love. "Is God able?" "Does God care?" The Bible answers both questions with a resounding "Yes!" God did not abandon the people beside the sea, nor did God leave them in the desert. Instead, because of God's great love and mighty power, the people arrived safely at God's abode on Mount Zion (15:13).

The curtain falls on this scene of Pharaoh's destruction with Miriam taking a timbrel (a small hand-drum) and leading the women in a victory dance. As they danced, they sang, "Sing to the Lord, for [the Lord] has triumphed gloriously; horse and rider [the Lord] has thrown into the sea" (15:21). Summing up the significance of these events, Fretheim wrote:

> The morning light breaks through the darkness, the people walk on dry land, God's just order is vindicated, and a new creation (v. 16) emerges into the brightness of a new day. It is called redemption (v. 13).[10]

Notes

[1]Brevard S. Childs, *The Book of Genesis* (Philadelphia: Westminster Press, 1974) 232.

[2]W. Gunther Plaut, *The Torah: A Modern Commentary* (New York: Union of American Hebrew Congregations, 1983) 3.

[3]Terrence E. Fretheim, *Exodus* (Louisville KY: John Knox Press, 1991) 110.

[4]J. Edgar Park, "Exodus," in *The Interpreter's Bible* (New York and Nashville: Abingdon- Cokesbury Press, 1952) 1:899-900.

[5]Ronald E. Clements, "Exodus," in *The Cambridge Bible Commentary* (Cambridge: Cambridge University Press, 1972) 65.

[6]Fretheim, 143.

[7]Childs, 238.

[8]Plaut, 149.

[9]Daniel D. Rhodes, *A Covenant Community* (Richmond VA: John Knox Press, 1964) 35.

[10]Fretheim, 169-70.

Chapter 5

Covenant and Commitment at Sinai
Exodus 15:22–20:21; 24:1–40:38

We turn now to the journey of the Israelites from the Red Sea to Sinai, the making of the covenant between God and Israel, and the building of the tabernacle according to the pattern revealed to Moses on the mountain. The legal sections in the book of Exodus, including the Ten Commandments (20:1-17) and the Book of the Covenant (20:22–23:33), will be dealt with in subsequent chapters.

The Road to Sinai

Israel's journey from the Red Sea to Sinai was anything but pleasant. Trouble began early with food and water shortages (15:22-27; 16:1-36; 17:1-7). As if this were not enough, Moses had to deal with a ferocious attack upon the Israelites from desert tribesmen called Amalekites (17:8-16).

The Israelites responded to the wilderness difficulties by complaining to God and murmuring against Moses (15:24; 16:2-3; 17:2-3). They had become so accustomed to having others take care of their needs while they were in Egypt that they were totally unprepared for their trek across the desert. Knight describes their problem:

> In this new life Israel must learn to stand upon her own feet; a clutter of slaves who were not allowed even to think for themselves have now to learn to be responsible, decision-making adults—and immediately they fail. Only Moses keeps his head, and keeps his faith.[1]

The Psalter gives a similar perspective on this period in Israel's history:

> How often they rebelled against him in the wilderness and grieved him in the desert! They tested God again and again, and provoked the Holy One of Israel. They did not keep in mind his power, or the day when he redeemed them from the foe; when he displayed his signs in Egypt, and his miracles in the fields of Zoan. (Ps 78:40-43)

The appalling thing about Israel's rebellion is that it happened on the heels of the miracle of deliverance at the Red Sea. On that occasion Israel had only to stand still and see the salvation of the Lord. The mighty forces of Pharaoh had been no match for Israel's defender. Even so, those who had been delivered from the jaws of death found it difficult to believe that God could supply their everyday needs for food, water, and protection. Instead of relying on God in simple trust, they lamented their meager desert diet and began to long for the abundant food supply they had left behind in Egypt (16:2-3).

The Israelites proved that they were ill-prepared to pay the price of freedom. It often is easier to get people out of slavery than to get slavery out of people. Slavery is dehumanizing, and its victims often lose the will to resist. It was only human for the Israelites to chafe under the rigors of desert living, but it was wrong for them to glamorize their past life of slavery in Egypt and long to return to it. They made such a fetish of survival that they wondered how they could exist apart from the life-giving waters of the Nile.

The price the Israelites had to pay for their rebellion in the wilderness, both before reaching Sinai and after leaving it, has been aptly described by the modern Jewish writer, Herman Wouk.

> The generation of Jews that Moses led into the desert collapsed into despair and panic over and over in moments of crises. Broken by slavery, they could not shake free of improvidence, cowardice, and idol worship. All the men who had been slaves in Egypt had to die in the desert, and a new generation had to take up their arms and their religion, before the Jews could cross the Jordan.[2]

Immediately after the Israelites reached Sinai, guests arrived in the camp. They included Jethro (Moses' father-in-law), Zipporah (Jethro's daughter and Moses' wife), and Moses' two sons by Zipporah (18:1-5). The account of Jethro's visit provides a delightful interlude in an otherwise stormy sequence of events in the Exodus story. By the time readers reach this point, they are likely to be emotionally exhausted. Eavesdropping on the conversation between Moses and his father-in-law provides a moment of welcome relief.

Moses invited Jethro into his tent and rehearsed to him all the good things that God had done for Israel since the last time they had met. Jethro was so impressed by what he heard that he made a threefold response. First, he blessed the God of Israel for blessings granted (18:10). Second, he confessed a newfound faith in Israel's God as greater than all other gods (18:11). His confession began with the familiar words, "Now I know" (See 1 Kgs 17:24; 2 Kgs 5:15). The confession indicates that Jethro had arrived at a new understanding of revelation based upon the Lord's mighty deeds. Third, Jethro presented burnt offerings and sacrifices to the Lord (18:12). One is impressed by the absence of any spirit of sectarianism in this passage. The writer does not tell us whether Jethro had previously known and worshiped the God of Moses or whether this represented his conversion experience. In any event, here was an outsider who confessed faith in the God of Israel and was accepted as a covenant-partner.

Jethro then observed how Moses spent the entire day ministering justice to the people of Israel (18:13-16). When Jethro saw that the workload Moses was carrying placed strain on him as well as placing strain on the people, Jethro offered some fatherly advice. He urged Moses to divide his judging responsibilities with others, keeping the major cases under his own jurisdiction and appointing assistants to handle the other cases. This arrangement would free up Moses' time for more important tasks, especially that of teaching the people the will of God (18:17-20).

Jethro mentioned four qualifications that Moses must look for in persons chosen to share his responsibilities (18:21). These qualifications would still be appropriate for persons seeking public office in our day. (1) They must be qualified for the job—"able." (2) They must be persons of reverence and true piety—"fear God." (3) They must be persons whose speech and behavior are governed by integrity and truthfulness—"trustworthy." (4) Public leaders should be impervious to bribery—"hate dishonest gain." Jethro's proposal called for these standards to be applied across the board, regardless of whether individuals were being appointed as officers over thousands, or hundreds, or fifties, or tens. This guaranteed the integrity of Israel's judicial system from top to bottom.

Moses welcomed the advice of Jethro and appointed the leaders he had suggested (18:24-26). Fleming James has summarized what this story reveals about the character of Moses: "The story illustrates three traits of Moses: his devotion to the people, his readiness to take advice, and his willingness to delegate authority."[3] Following his brief visit with Moses, Jethro returned to his own land (18:27). He did not accompany the Israelites on their journey to Canaan, although other members of his family did so (Jgs 1:16).

Covenant and Commitment at Sinai

Moses finally arrived at the place where God first spoke to him, and he had his proof that God had indeed sent him to deliver the Israelites (see 3:12). Before the liberated slaves could go on their way to receive the land promised to their ancestors, their relationship to God had to be sealed by a solemn covenant. The place we call Sinai is known today as Jebel Musa, Arabic for "Mountain of Moses." It lies some fifty-five miles north from the southern tip of the Sinai Peninsula. It rises 7,467 feet above sea level and stands 2,600 feet above the surrounding plateau. It can be scaled in approximately one and one-half hours. The Israelites remained encamped at this spot for almost a year (see Num 10:11-12), during which time three significant events took place: (1) The Israelites were granted a vision of God similar to what Moses had received on an earlier occasion (see 3:1-6); (2) a covenant was established between God and the people; and (3) the law was given to guide the people in their covenant responsibilities.

The Meaning of Covenant

The Hebrew word for covenant (*berith*) occurs more than 280 times in the Hebrew Scriptures. Its basic meaning is "bond" or "fetter." A covenant, therefore, is a binding contract or treaty. Covenants could be made between two individuals, as in the case of David and Jonathan (1 Sam 18:1-4), or between two tribes or nations, as in the case of the Israelites and the Gibeonites (Josh 9:3-27). The parties to a treaty could be on an equal footing, or one could be subordinate to the other. The covenant between Jacob and Laban (Gen 31:43-54) was a covenant between equals, otherwise known as a parity treaty. A covenant between unequals, as in the case of a king and his conquered subjects, was known as a vassal treaty. The covenant between God and Israel was more like a vassal treaty than a parity treaty. It imposed duties and restrictions upon Israel but in no way restricted God. It was offered to Israel as an undeserved benefit and honor.

The Process of Covenant Making at Sinai

The making of the covenant at Sinai took place in six stages: God's invitation, preparation of the people, the appearance of God, the proclamation of the Ten Commandments, Moses' appointment as mediator, and the sealing of the covenant.

(1) *God's invitation to the people to enter into the covenant relationship and their ready response* (19:1-9). Soon after Israel arrived at Sinai, Moses climbed the mountain to receive God's message and returned to deliver it to the people. It began by reminding the people of how God has rescued them from the Egyptians and had borne them as on eagles' wings to bring them into the divine presence (19:3-4). The message concluded with an invitation and a promise. God said, "If you obey my voice and keep my covenant, you shall be my treasured possession out of all of the peoples. Indeed, the whole earth is mine, but you shall be for me a priestly kingdom and a holy nation" (19:5-6a).

The phrase "treasured possession" is a translation of the Hebrew term *segullah*. This word occurs only eight times in the Hebrew Scriptures, twice with reference to the treasured possession of a king (1 Chron 29:3; Eccl 2:8), and six times in symbolic reference to Israel as the treasured possession of God (Exod 19:5; Deut 7:6; 14:2; 26:18; Ps 135:4; Mal 3:17). The term passed over into the New Testament by way of the Septuagint and came to be used to describe the Christians' unique relationship to God through Jesus Christ (see Eph 1:14; 2 Thess 2:14; Titus 2:14; 1 Pet 2:9). It is important to note that in God's choice of Israel as God's treasured possession, God did not relinquish claim on other nations, for God emphatically states, "Indeed, the whole earth is mine" (19:5b). Abraham had first been called to be a blessing to all nations (Gen 12:1-3), and that mission was now being transferred to the whole nation of Israel.

The second term used to spell out Israel's mission under the covenant is "a priestly kingdom" (19:6a). This term occurs only here in the Hebrew Scriptures, but is translated "a royal priesthood" in 1 Peter 2:9, and "a kingdom and priests" in Revelation 5:10, both passages applying the term to the unique relationship of the church to Jesus Christ (also see Rev 1:6; 20:6). The use of "priestly kingdom" in its original setting meant that Israel was to perform a priestly function to the nations comparable to what the Levitical priests performed to the tribes of Israel. This would involve offering prayers and sacrifices on behalf of the nations and instructing them in the ways of the Lord. The primary emphasis in this verse, therefore, is upon missionary outreach.

The third phrase used to describe what Israel was to become under the covenant is "a holy nation" (19:6b), that is, a nation set apart from all other nations as belonging exclusively to God. This means that the mission of Israel was ultimately rooted and grounded in character. Israel could not be a priestly nation unless it had first become a holy nation. Holiness and vocation must always be inseparably linked in the lives of God's people.

Israel's special vocation was not to be forced, but left to free choice. Therefore, when Moses came down from the mountain, he assembled the elders of the people and set before them the demands of the covenant (19:7). They had to decide whether or not they wished to proceed further with this matter. The people's response was enthusiastically affirmative: "Everything that the Lord has spoken we will do" (19:8b). It was a covenant freely offered and freely accepted.

(2) *The preparation of the people for their encounter with the Lord* (19:10-15). Moses commanded the people to spend two days consecrating themselves in preparation for their encounter with God. They

were to wash their garments and to make sure they kept their distance from the sacred mountain. Only when the trumpet sounded a long blast were they to venture near (19:13).

(3) *The awesome appearance of God on the third day* (19:16-25). When the people gathered at the foot of the mountain on the third day, it was a moment of great suspense. They watched as Moses slowly scaled the mountain to meet God. Moses' ascent was undertaken amidst a display of thunder, lightning, earthquake, trumpet, fire, and smoke. All of nature was in an upheaval at this divine-human encounter. When the trumpet reached its highest pitch, Moses began to speak with God, and God answered him in thunderclaps. Armed with a fresh message from God, Moses descended the mountain to address the people (19:21-25).

(4) *The proclamation of the Ten Commandments, the foundational law of the covenant* (20:1-17). The Ten Commandments provide only the basic framework of biblical law. For instance, they forbid the worship of other gods, but do not specify how Israel's God is to be worshiped. They condemn stealing, but do not specify how thieves are to be dealt with. In a sense, therefore, the remaining legal portions of the Hebrew Scriptures are but a supplement to the Ten Commandments, an attempt to apply these basic principles to all areas of life —the home, the courts, the marketplace, and the temple.

Although the majority of these commandments are expressed negatively—"Thou shalt not"—biblical scholars have been quick to point out that their negative form does not imply a negative attitude toward life. On the contrary, they are designed to protect and enrich life. This truth was emphasized by David H. C. Read in a sermon entitled " 'Thou Shalt Not!'—Says Who?" in which he discussed the relevance of these ancient laws. He took note of the fact that many today regard the Ten Commandments as totally outdated. The most that modern society would be disposed to accept would be Ten Suggestions. According to Read,

> A lot of nonsense has been written about the oppressive and negative nature of such provisions [as one finds in the Ten Commandments]. In fact, "Thou shalt not!" is a far easier path than "Thou shalt." Tell me there is one thing I may not do, and you leave me free to enjoy a thousand other things. Those who abandon all moral restraint are notoriously the most distracted and miserable men and women. Is the observance of the Ten Commandments really a terrible burden for a normal human being? Don't you think you could have a wonderful day without having to kill, steal, lie, or commit adultery?[4]

The preamble to the Ten Commandments (20:2) shows that these laws were predicated upon God's gracious act of deliverance in bringing Israel out of Egypt. To cite the commandments apart from the preamble is to distort their meaning. God is presented in the preamble not as a tyrant but as a liberator. In giving the Ten Commandments, therefore, God was not seeking to place the Israelites under a new form of bondage, but to establish guidelines to safeguard their liberty and to enhance their well-being. Those who look to God as the author of their freedom will never find God's service painful or burdensome.

(5) *Moses' appointment as mediator between God and the Israelites* (20:18-21). Reference already has been made to the high drama being played out on the mountain as Moses addressed God and was answered by successive claps of thunder (19:19). When the people waiting below could no longer stand the tension, they broke and ran to what they considered to be a safe distance from the mountain (20:18). In order to avoid such terrifying encounters with God in the future, they approached Moses upon his return and made an urgent request of him. They asked that from then on he should receive the word of God and bring it to them, but that God should not speak to them directly as God had done at Sinai (20:19). This request was somewhat of a watershed in Hebrew religion, for it marked the first time the Israelites had expressed a felt need to have someone serve as mediator between them and God. The office of prophet was created in part to meet this need (see Deut 18:15-18). From this moment onward there is no record of God having spoken to an Israelite assembly except through a messenger. The office of mediator was ultimately fulfilled through Jesus Christ (1 Tim 2:5).

(6) *The sealing of the covenant* (24:1-18). The covenant-making ceremony was finalized by the events described in chapter 24. First, preparations were made for Moses, Aaron, Nadab, Abihu, and the seventy elders of Israel to go up the mountain to meet the Lord (24:1-2). Before they set out on their journey, a covenant affirmation ceremony was held at the foot of the mountain, during which the people renewed their pledge to observe all that the Lord has spoken (24:3-8). Finally, after Moses and his companions had reached an appointed place somewhere up the side of Sinai, they stopped to share a meal in the presence of God (24:9-11). By eating and drinking before God, the representatives of Israel were formally accepting on behalf of all the people the obligations of the covenant. It would be difficult to exaggerate the significance of this solemn occasion. Israel was now pledged to serve the Lord in perpetuity. The Lord's Supper has something of this same significance for Christians.

After this shared meal and final confirmation of the covenant, Moses was summoned to the top of Sinai to receive the Ten Commandments. These laws previously had been delivered by Moses to the people in oral form (20:1-17), but were now to be engraved upon two tablets of stone (24:12-18). While on the mountain, Moses heard God speaking out of the cloud (v. 16). He remained there with God forty days and forty nights (v. 18). Moses' prolonged absence set the stage for Israel's rebellion against the Lord in the golden calf episode.

The Breaking of the Covenant
31:18–32:25

George Ernest Wright often told his students at Harvard that the only covenant Israel ever knew was a broken covenant. During the forty days Moses spent on the mountain receiving the tablets of the law and instructions for constructing the tabernacle, the people grew tired of waiting for him. Fearful that Moses had disappeared forever, they set about devising a way to worship the "gods" they supposed had delivered them out of Egypt (32:1). They seem to have had the support of Aaron as they developed their plans. He was willing to collect their offerings of gold, mold them into the image of a calf, build an altar, and offer sacrifices to their newly adopted gods (32:2-6). It is recorded that the people "sat down to eat and drink, and then gave themselves up to revelry" (v. 6b, NEB).

What could have been a high moment in the spiritual history of Israel turned out to be a time of national apostasy. The Israelites quickly abandoned the God who had freed them from the power of Pharaoh. Before Moses returned with the tablets inscribed with the Ten Commandments, Israel had already broken the first of these by setting up other gods in the place of the true God. If God had permitted this to go unpunished, Israel's religion would have degenerated to the level of that of its pagan neighbors. The remainder of the Bible shows how God maintained this covenant—this broken covenant—even in the face of Israel's failure and infidelity.

The Lord urged Moses to make haste and return to the camp of the Israelites, saying to him, "Your people, whom you brought up out of the land of Egypt, have acted perversely" (32:7). Note the change between these words and those found in the preamble to the Ten Commandments, "I am the Lord your God, who brought you up out of the land of Egypt, out of the house of slavery" (20:2). It was as if God had decided to disown the Israelites because they were in open rebellion against God. God even threatened to blot them out and make a new beginning with Moses, similar to the new beginning that God had made with Noah and his family (32:9-10).

Other persons might have been flattered at such an offer, but not Moses. He made intercession for the people of Israel to prevent God from destroying them. He made a two-pronged appeal on their behalf. The first appeal was to God's reputation among the heathen if Israel were allowed to be destroyed (32:11-12). Moses also appealed to God to remember the promises made to Israel's ancestors, Abraham, Isaac, and (Jacob) Israel (32:13). The fervent prayer of Moses altered the situation and made God willing to give the Israelites a second chance (32:14).

The discovery that the people had made a golden calf caused Moses to smash the two tablets of the law (32:15-19). He then caused the golden calf to be melted in the fire, had it ground into powder, and mixed it with the people's drinking water (32:20). This may have been intended as a form of trial by ordeal in which those who drank the water would die if guilty but would suffer no harm if innocent (see Num 5:11-28).

Still, the people had to be punished for their apostasy. Moses issued a call for any who were on the Lord's side to come over to him (32:25-26). The sons of Levi were among those who rallied to Moses' side (v. 26), and they were sent throughout the camp to put the rebels to the sword (32:27). The number of those slain is given as 3,000 (32:28), although the Vulgate reads 23,000, perhaps influenced by 1 Corinthians 10:8. The Levites received a special blessing for their loyalty to God and to God's servant, Moses (32:29).

Chapter 32 concludes with one of the greatest prayers of intercession found in the Bible (vv. 30-35). Moses freely acknowledges Israel's sin but begs God for forgiveness. He claims no right to make such a petition, but offers his life as a substitute for their lives. It is a sign of his greatness that he was willing to die for those who had distrusted him and accused him of bringing them into the wilderness to perish. This prayer stood without parallel until one greater than Moses came and prayed, "Father, forgive them; for they do not know what they are doing" (Luke 23:34).

The Covenant Renewed

34:1-35

Chapter 34 is a continuation of chapter 32. It describes the renewal of the covenant following the golden calf incident. The Lord told Moses to cut two stone tablets like those he had broken and bring them to the top of the mountain to be inscribed with a new copy of the commandments (34:1-3). After Moses had climbed the mountain, the Lord descended in a cloud to meet him. Moses was then given a proclamation of the divine name and an interpretation of its meaning:

> The Lord, the Lord, a God merciful and gracious, slow to anger, and abounding in steadfast love and faithfulness, keeping steadfast love for the thousandth generation, forgiving iniquity and transgression and sin, yet by no means clearing the guilty, but visiting the iniquity of the parents upon the children and the children's children, to the third and the fourth generation. (34:6-7)

These verses furnish a clear statement of Israel's covenant theology. They give a balanced view of God's sovereignty and Israel's freedom and responsibility. Moses' response to God's self-revelation served as a model for all future generations of Israelite worshipers: "And Moses quickly bowed his head toward the earth, and worshiped" (34:8). He also uttered a bold request that the Lord might accompany this stiff-necked people on their journey from Sinai (34:9). The Lord's response was an announcement of the renewal of the covenant (34:10).

When Moses rejoined the Israelites at the foot of the mountain, his face radiated with rays of light, a reflection of the fact that he had been talking with God (34:29-35). The Hebrew for "rays" of light means literally "horns" of light. When Jerome translated the Hebrew text into the Latin of the Vulgate version, he made a literal rendering of verse 29, causing it to be read: "And Moses did not know that the skin of his face was horned because of his conversation with the Lord." Due to the influence of this translation, Michelangelo later produced his famous sculpture of Moses with horns protruding from Moses' forehead. Thus, a mistranslation was forever set in stone!

God's Presence with God's Pilgrim People
33:1–40:38

A review of the chronology of the Exodus events will give us a better understanding of the concluding chapters of the book of Exodus.

- The Exodus occurred on the fourteenth day of the first month of the year of Israel's liberation (12:2-6, 17-18).
- Three months later the people reached Sinai (19:1).
- After three days the covenant-making ceremony got under way (19:16).
- After the covenant had been confirmed, Moses was summoned to the top of Sinai, where he remained forty days. While there he

received the tablets of the law and detailed instructions for building the tabernacle and organizing the worship of Israel (24:15–31:18).

- Moses' prolonged stay on the mountain convinced the people that he had disappeared forever, and this led to their turning to the worship of the golden calf (32:1-35).
- After God had punished the people for their apostasy, God summoned Moses back to the top of Sinai for another stint of forty days, during which time the tablets of law were rewritten and the covenant was renewed (34:1-35).
- Coming down the mountain again, Moses assembled the people and gave them final instructions for building of the tabernacle (35:1-19).
- The people enthusiastically set to work and finished the tabernacle and its furnishings on the first day of the first month of the second year of their liberation (40:17).
- On the twentieth day of the following month they took their leave of Sinai and headed for Canaan, ending an eleven-month sojourn (see Num 10:11-12).

Some might ask why it was so important to the Israelites to spend those months building a tabernacle to take with them across the desert. The Israelites themselves would never have raised this question. After all, had they not left the "service" of Pharaoh to engage in the "service" (worship) of God in the wilderness? Those who had been forced to build store cities for Pharaoh joyfully and willingly spent almost a year building a tabernacle for the Lord. The building of the tabernacle also resolved what had become a pressing problem for the people. Since Sinai was the place where they had met God and established a covenant with God, how would they maintain contact with this God after they left Sinai and headed north? Would they have to make annual pilgrimages back to the place of God's dwelling at Sinai?

Moses dared to hope that God's presence might go with the Israelites wherever they went. He gave classic expression to his hope in these words:

> If your presence will not go, do not carry us up from here. For how shall it be known that I have found favor in your sight, I and your people, unless you go with us? In this way, we shall be distinct, I and your people, from every people on the face of the earth. (33:15-16)

God responded to Moses' request by permitting the construction of the tabernacle. The prevailing view of the Hebrew Scriptures is that while God dwells permanently in heaven, God "tabernacles" or "tents" on earth. The portable desert tent embodied this idea. Sinai had its limitations, for there *only Moses* was permitted to meet with God. Now, however, the Lord God was willing to tabernacle in the midst of a people on the move. In the words of Martin Buber, Israel's God was "a great deity of the road."[5]

After the tabernacle had been completed, all that remained to be done was for God's glory to descend upon it! The Bible describes this momentous event in these words: "Then the cloud covered the tent of meeting, and the glory of the Lord filled the tabernacle" (40:34). The significance of God's presence in the tabernacle has been underscored by Mann:

> Without that presence, the tabernacle is no more than an empty shell, devoid of any theological significance. Thus the enthronement of Yahweh in [the Lord's] tabernacle constitutes the climax of the book, and indeed of the Pentateuchal narrative up to this point. . . . In the context of the Pentateuchal narrative, the enthronement of the covenant Lord of Israel in the tent of meeting provides a community of God and humankind that the world has not seen since the first man and woman were driven from Eden.[6]

The theology of the tabernacling presence of God is reflected in what John wrote about the Incarnation: "So the Word became flesh; he came to dwell among us, and we saw his glory, such glory as befits the Father's only Son, full of grace and truth" (John 1:14, NEB).

Notes

[1]George A. F. Knight, *Theology as Narrative* (Grand Rapids: Eerdmans, 1976) 112.

[2]Herman Wouk, *This Is My God* (Garden City: Doubleday, 1959) 72-73.

[3]Fleming James, *Personalities of the Old Testament* (New York: Charles Scribner's Sons, 1951) 25.

[4]David H. C. Read, " 'Thou Shalt Not!'—Says Who?" *The Expository Times*, vol. 88.7 (April 1977): 210-211.

[5]Martin Buber, *The Prophetic Faith* (New York: Harper & Row, 1949) 42.

[6]Thomas W. Mann, *The Book of the Torah* (Atlanta: John Knox Press, 1988) 112.

Chapter 6

Covenant and Law

Exodus 20–23; Leviticus 1–27

M ost of the legal material in the Pentateuch is clustered in Exodus
20–40; Leviticus 1–27; Numbers 1:1–10:10; and Deuteronomy
1–33. The Ten Commandments (Exod 20:1-17; Deut 5:6-21) and the
remainder of Deuteronomy will be treated in the final chapter of this
study. Attention here will be focused on the Book of the Covenant
(Exod 20:22–23:33) and Leviticus 1–26.

Christians are not likely to get very excited about studying the
legal material in the Hebrew Scriptures. Many suspect that these
ancient laws are not relevant to the contemporary world. Paul's affirmation that we are not under law but under grace (Rom 6:14) has led
to widespread neglect, if not outright repudiation, of the law. My position in this chapter is the opposite of this. I will try to show that the
study of the law can provide positive benefits, even for the Christian.

Gospel and law, rightly understood, are not opposed to each other.
Both are gifts from God. Paul recognized this fact when he described
the blessings he had received from his Jewish ancestors. He wrote,

> They are Israelites, and to them belong the adoption, the glory, the
> covenants, the giving of the law, the worship, and the promises; to
> them belong the patriarchs, and from them, according to the flesh,
> comes the Messiah, who is over all, God blessed forever. Amen.
> (Rom 9:4-5)

We would be wide off the mark to suppose that the people of the
Hebrew Scriptures regarded the law as an unbearable burden. Otherwise, how are we to explain the many passages found in the Hebrew
Scriptures that praise the law as an unparalleled blessing? Consider,
for example, Deuteronomy 6:20-25.

> When your son [or daughter] asks you in time to come, "What is the
> meaning of the precepts, statutes, and laws which the Lord our God
> gave you?" you shall say to him [and her], "We were Pharaoh's slaves
> in Egypt, and the Lord brought us out of Egypt with [the Lord's]
> strong hand, sending great disasters, signs, and portents against the
> Egyptians and against Pharaoh and all his family, as we saw for
> ourselves. But [the Lord] led us out from there to bring us into the
> land and give it to us as [the Lord] had promised to our forefathers.
> The Lord commanded us to observe all these statutes and to fear the

Lord our God; it will be for our own good at all times, and [the Lord] will continue to preserve our lives. It will be counted to our credit if we keep all these commandments in the sight of the Lord our God, as [God] has bidden us." (NEB)

Those who study the book of Psalms soon discover that one of its constant themes is thanksgiving for the law. Psalm 1 pronounces a benediction on those whose delight is in the law of the Lord and who meditate on its teachings day and night (v. 2). Psalm 119 is an alphabetic poem of twenty-two stanzas, one for each of the twenty-two letters of the Hebrew alphabet. Each stanza, in turn, is made up of eight verses, and each verse in a given stanza begins with the letter of the alphabet that corresponds to that stanza. The stanzas run through the entire Hebrew alphabet from *aleph* to *tav*, or, as we would say, from *a* to *z*. The theme of this psalm is the surpassing excellence of the law. One has only to read this lengthy poem to realize what joy and delight faithful Israelites felt when they studied the law! They could declare with deep sincerity: "Oh, how I love thy law! It is my meditation all day long" (v. 97; see also Ps 19:7-11).

The New Testament further describes the law's contribution to the Christian. Galatians 3:19-24 explains how the law served as custodian to bring us to Christ. Paul also believed that the law was given to help people understand the true nature of sin and, thus, be able to recognize their need for forgiveness (see Rom 3:19-20; 7:7-12). Jesus stated his support for the law when he said, "Think not that I have come to abolish the law and the prophets; I have not come to abolish them but to fulfil them. For truly, I say to you, till heaven and earth pass away, not an iota, not a dot, will pass away until all is accomplished" (Matt 5:17-18 RSV). Jesus then proceeded to illustrate what he meant by reinterpreting some of the key stipulations of the law of the Hebrew Scriptures in the light of the Gospel (Matt 5:21-22, 27-28, 38-42). In each of these instances, Jesus took a law from the Hebrew Scriptures and increased its authority and significance by internalizing it. Thus, Jesus broadened the law's demands upon the lives of his followers. To be sure, Jesus was not a legalist in his application of the law. He was always ready to set aside a particular law, such as the law of the Sabbath, in order to fulfill a higher law. Still, Jesus never gave his followers permission to ignore the righteous demands of the law. We are the losers when we forget this.

The Book of the Covenant
Exodus 20:22–23:33

Standing immediately after the Ten Commandments is a block of legal material known as the "Book of the Covenant." This name can be traced back to Exodus 24:7, where it is stated that Moses "took the book of the covenant, and read it in the hearing of the people; and they said, 'All that the Lord has spoken we will do, and we will be obedient.' " This is perhaps the oldest law code in the Hebrew Scriptures and one of the earliest to have circulated among ancient peoples. It preceded Roman law codes by at least a thousand years. Its deep concern for morality and justice influenced the development of all subsequent law codes in ancient Israel.

The Book of the Covenant may be outlined as follows:

I. Laws Regulating Worship (20:22-26)
II. Laws Protecting Human Rights (21:1-32)
III. Laws Protecting Property Rights (21:33–22:17)
IV. Miscellaneous Social and Religious Laws (22:18–23:9)
V. A Calendar of Religious Festivals (23:10-19)
VI. Concluding Warnings and Exhortation (23:20-23)

We may note some of the unique features of this code of law. One is its broad humanitarian spirit. Its first laws protecting human rights are concerned with the rights of slaves (21:1-11). No other nation in antiquity besides Israel is known to have had laws designed to insure the kindly treatment of its slaves. The Book of the Covenant even assumes that slaves may be given their freedom under certain circumstances.

The law of retaliation is another example of the humane nature of this code (see 21:23-25). Of course, we do not normally think of the principle of "an eye for an eye" and "a tooth for a tooth" as falling in the category of humane legislation. But rightly understood, it is exactly that, for it served to limit the scope of the punishment that could be meted out to an offender by establishing the principle that punishment for an injury inflicted on another should correspond in degree and in kind to the injury. We recognize, however, that Jesus articulated a higher law for Christian "retaliations" (see Matt 5:38-42).

Other defenseless members of society were also protected by the regulations of this code. Twice it reminds Israelites not to harm aliens residing in their midst, remembering that they once were aliens in the land of Egypt (22:21; 23:9). Slaves and aliens were also to be allowed to rest and refresh themselves on the Sabbath (23:12). Further defense of the rights of aliens can be found in Leviticus 19:33-34 and 23:22, and in Numbers 9:14 and 15:14-16. Commenting on the appeal to the Israelites to show mercy toward aliens because they themselves once were aliens in Egypt, Fretheim wrote, "When the people of God mistreat the poor, they violate their own history. It is not simply a violation of the laws of God; more fundamentally, it is disavowal of their own past, of those salvific acts which made them what they [are]."[1]

Widows, orphans, and the poor were also protected by the provision of the Book of the Covenant (22:22-24). Lenders were commanded not to charge interest on loans they made to the poor (22:25). Furthermore, if a lender took a poor person's garment as security for a loan, the garment was to be returned at sundown so the owner could cover himself with it during the night (22:26-27).

The humanitarian spirit in the Book of the Covenant is further reinforced by a demand for justice in all human relationships Exodus 23:1-3 reads:

> You shall not spread a false report. You shall not join hands with the wicked to act as a malicious witness. You shall not follow a majority in wrongdoing; when you bear witness in a lawsuit, you shall not side with the majority so as to pervert justice; nor shall you be partial to the poor in a lawsuit.

In other words, justice must not be denied to anyone, including the rich. Consider also 23:6-8.

> You shall not pervert the justice due to your poor in their lawsuits. Keep far from a false charge, and do not kill the innocent and those in the right, for I will not acquit the guilty. You shall take no bribe, for a bribe blinds the officials, and subverts the cause of those who are in the right.

These verses should make us more concerned about abuses in our own legal system.

The main attention of the Book of the Covenant is focused on matters of worship. It seeks to safeguard the worship of the one true God by prohibiting the making of other gods (20:23). Idolatry is regarded as a serious offense, punishable by death (22:20; 23:13). Sabbath observance is required of all members of the Israelite community, including slaves and resident aliens (23:12). All males are commanded to come to the Lord's sanctuary three times each year (23:14). The three pilgrimages were for the purpose of observing the three principle religious festivals of the year: the combined spring festival of Passover and Unleavened Bread (23:15); the summer festival of wheat harvest, or Pentecost (23:16a); and the autumn festival of ingathering, or Tabernacles (23:16b).

The Book of the Covenant concludes with a list of blessings promised to Israel if the people remain obedient (23:20-33). Similar lists are found at the end of law codes in Leviticus 26:3-13 and in Deuteronomy 28:1-14. Included among the blessings listed here are the protection and guidance of a guardian angel on Israel's journey from Sinai to Canaan (23:20-22); victory for Israel over all of its enemies (23:23-24, 27-33); and the threefold blessing of prosperity, health, and long life (23:25-26).

The Law of Leviticus

The title for the book of Leviticus in the Hebrew Bible is the first word of the Hebrew text, a verb form that would be translated, "And [the Lord] called." The Septuagint, the oldest Greek translation of the Hebrew Scriptures, calls this book *Levitikon*, and the Latin Vulgate adapts this to read *Liber Leviticus*, that is, "the Levitical Book." The English title comes from the Vulgate. It is not a very satisfactory title, since the Levites play a very minor role in the book, being mentioned in only one brief passage, and then only with reference to their property rights (25:32-33). Levi, the ancestor of the priests and Levites, is never mentioned at all.

Leviticus opens with a reference to the voice of the Lord coming to Moses from the tabernacle (1:1), thus linking Leviticus to the last chapter of Exodus. All of Leviticus, as well as the priestly law found in Numbers 1:1–10:10, is said to have been communicated to Moses before the Israelites left Sinai. The overall aim of Leviticus is best expressed in 20:26: "You shall be holy to me; for I the Lord am holy, and I have separated you from the other peoples to be mine" (see also 11:44-45; 19:2; 20:7-8). To be holy means "to be separated or set apart as belonging to the Lord." According to the Scriptures, a place becomes holy when it is set apart from ordinary places and dedicated exclusively to God. Likewise, a day becomes holy when it belongs to God. Persons also become holy by belonging to the holy God. Holiness, therefore, is not an intrinsic quality of persons, places, or times, but a quality conferred upon them because of their unique relationship to God. Only contact with the holy God can make something else holy.

Laws Concerning Sacrifices (1:1–7:38)

The instructions given in 1:1–7:38 apply not only to the worshipers bringing sacrificial offerings to the sanctuary (1:1–6:7), but also to the priests officiating at the altars of sacrifice (6:8–7:38). Some sacrifices were offered spontaneously, while others were decreed by God and necessary for dealing with the problems of sin and guilt. The voluntary offerings included burnt offerings, grain offerings, and peace offerings. The mandatory offerings were the sin offerings and the guilt offerings.

(1) *The burnt offering* (1:1-17; 6:8-13). This offering is called by a variety of names in modern translations of the Bible. These names include "whole offering" (NEB) and "holocaust" (JB). The burnt offering was burnt on the altar as a gift to God and as an act of praise and adoration. The animal for the burnt offering had to be a male without blemish chosen from the worshiper's flock or herd (1:3). As a concession to those too poor to afford an animal, a turtledove or pigeon might be substituted (1:14-17). After the sacrificial animal (or bird) had been cleaned and dressed and its blood sprinkled on the sides of the altar (1:5, 11, 15), it was reduced to ashes by the fire on the altar. Neither the worshipers nor the priests were allowed to eat any of the flesh.

The smoke of the burnt offering is described as "a pleasing odor to the Lord" (1:9, 13, 17; see Gen 8:20-21). The blessing sought by one making a burnt offering might be summed up by the word "atonement," that is, "at-one-ment" with God (1:4). A burnt offering might be offered on such occasions as a time of crisis (1 Sam 13:8-10), the dedication of an altar (Jgs 6:25-26), the dedicatory service for the temple (1 Kgs 8:64), or to accompany the prayer of a father for his children (Job 1:5). This offering was customarily accompanied by grain and drink offerings (Num 15:1-10). Finally, it should be noted that the burnt offering, with its emphasis on total surrender to God, was chosen as the daily public offering in Israel, the well-known "regular" or "continual" burnt offering (Exod 29:42; Num 28:1-8).

(2) *The grain offering* (2:1-16; 6:14-23). Other designations used for this offering are "meal offering" (KJV) and "cereal offering" (RSV). The Hebrew word refers to a tribute gift, such as a servant might give to his master, or a subject to his king, or a daughter to her mother. Tribute gifts might be given for a variety of purposes, such as seeking reconciliation (Gen 32:13-20), showing respect to a superior (1 Kgs 4:21), winning favor with another (Gen 43:11-15), or demonstrating one's loyalty (2 Kgs 17:3-4). Perhaps all these motives were involved in the presentation of grain offerings to the Lord. There is,

however, no mention of atonement or the need for forgiveness in connection with this offering.

Flour was the main ingredient of the grain offering. Before being cooked, it was mixed with oil, frankincense, and salt (2:1, 13). Leaven and honey, both of which promoted fermentation and decay in foods, were not to be added to the grain offerings (2:11). A handful of the flour of the grain offering was burned on the altar as a "token portion" for the Lord (2:2, 9, 16). The remainder was then cooked in one of the designated ways and given as food to the Aaronite priests (2:10).

(3) *The shared offering* (3:1-17; 7:11-36). Translators have had difficulty agreeing on a suitable name for this type of sacrifice. The Hebrew name is *shelamim*, the plural form of *shalom*, "peace," or "well-being." This is how the King James Version came to translate it as "peace offering." Most modern translations have abandoned this translation in favor of others, such as "offering of well-being" (NRSV), "shared offering" (NEB), "fellowship offering" (TEV), or "communion sacrifice" (JB). The Jewish scholar, Levine, has cited evidence from other Semitic languages that the peace offering represented a gift offered when one person greeted another or was welcomed into the presence of another. Levine, therefore, calls this "a sacred gift of greeting," rather than a "peace offering."[2]

The normal occasion for this type of offering was when family members and friends gathered to eat a fellowship meal and to rejoice before the Lord (see 1 Sam 9:11-14, 22-24; Deut 12:5-6). It was also utilized for public celebrations (see Lev 23:4-6, 19), as well as for special dedications and convocations (see Exod 24:3-5; Deut 27:1-8; 1 Sam 11:14-15; 1 Kgs 8:62-66).

The shared offering (peace offering) seems to have been the most joyous of all the sacrifices. It provided an occasion for worshipers to celebrate their sharing of a life of *shalom*, which included national stability, economic security, good health, and overall well-being. The note of joy was so prominent on such occasions that those in mourning were not expected to participate (see Deut 26:14; Isa 22:12-14). Shared offerings were designed to mark happy occasions in life, rather than to obtain forgiveness for any prior act of sin. This dispels the notion that the ancient Israelites embraced a joyless religion.

The animals slain for the shared offering might be either cattle (Lev 3:1-5), sheep (3:6-11), or goats (3:12-17). Both male and female animals were acceptable (3:1, 6), which was not the case with the burnt offering (1:3, 10). The flesh of this offering was shared by the priests and the people alike, and, in a figurative sense, by God as well. God's portion consisted of the blood, the fat, the kidneys, and the liver (3:2-4). After the blood had been sprinkled against the sides of the altar, the other parts were burnt upon the altar as a token burnt offering to the Lord (3:5, 11, 16). In the distribution of the flesh of the sacrificial animal, the priests received a choice portion known as the "elevation (or wave) offering" (7:30). The name suggests that the priests elevated their portion as if offering it to God and then receiving it back again.

It was considered meritorious to invite the poor to share in these fellowship meals (see Deut 14:28-29; 2 Sam 6:17-19; Luke 14:12-14). One is reminded of the exhortation of Hebrews 13:2: "Do not neglect to show hospitality to strangers, for by doing that some have entertained angels without knowing it."

(4) *The sin offering* (4:1–5:13; 6:24-30; Num 15:22-31). "Sin offering" is a somewhat misleading title for this sacrifice. It was not designed to solve the problem of sin as we understand it, but to safeguard the sanctity of the sanctuary against persons who were ritually unclean or who had carelessly or accidentally committed acts of desecration. Some, therefore, call this a "purification offering," or "a purgation offering." One might compare this with Jesus' "cleansing" the temple of merchants and moneychangers (Matt 21:12-13) or with the concern of Paul's enemies that Paul might have desecrated the temple by bringing Greeks into its sacred precincts (Acts 21:27-28). This is something that present-day Christians may have difficulty understanding, since we seldom assign any notion of special holiness to our church buildings.

The sin offering was required of anyone who had participated "unwittingly" in any of the things the Lord had commanded not to be done (4:2). It thus applied to inadvertent or unintentional sins committed by either the chief priest (4:1-12), the whole congregation of Israel (4:13-21), the ruler (4:22-26), or the individual citizen (4:27-34). A sin offering might be required to cleanse or purify a woman after childbirth (Lev 12:1-8; see Luke 2:22-24), or a person with leprosy or some other skin disease (Lev 13:1–14:32), or a house with mold or fungus in its walls [!] (14:33-53), or a person who has a bodily discharge (Lev 15:1-33), or a new altar about to be dedicated (Lev 8:14-17; Ezek 43:18-27).

All of the problems dealt with by means of the sin offering were ritual in nature, and not ethical or moral. Furthermore, only defilement unwittingly or accidentally acquired, such as coming near a corpse while under a vow (Num 6:1-12), could be removed by sacrificing a sin offering. There was no sacrifice for the person guilty of premeditated or intentional sins (see Num 15:27-31; 1 Sam 3:14; Heb 10:4, 26-27). In effect, the elaborate sacrificial system of the Hebrew

Scriptures seems to have arrived at an impasse, for it offered no solution for the sins that cried out most for forgiveness.

(5) *The guilt offering* (Lev 5:14–6:7; 7:1-7). The distinction between the sin offering and the guilt offering is somewhat blurred. As early as the time of Josephus (Ant. 3.9.3), Jewish scholars had difficulty distinguishing between the two. The Bible sometimes seems to use the two terms interchangeably (Lev 5:6, 7; compare 4:13-14 with 5:17-19). There is a difference between the stated purpose behind the two. The sin offering is designed to remove ritual defilement, thus safeguarding the sanctity of worship. The guilt offering, on the other hand, is for the purpose of righting a wrong or making amends for an injury. For this reason, the guilt offering is sometimes referred to as a "compensation offering," or a "reparation offering."[3]

Examples of situations that might require a guilt offering are given in Leviticus 5:14–6:7. The first case is that of someone who "unintentionally" withholds the Lord's "holy things" (v. 15). The "holy things" are not defined, although they may refer to tithes and offerings that have been kept back (see Mal 3:8-10; Acts 5:1-11). Forgiveness in this case required the presentation of a ram as a guilt offering (Lev 5:15), the restoration of the holy things that had been withheld (5:16a), and the payment of a penalty equal to one-fifth of that which was withheld (5:16b). Only then could the offender receive forgiveness for the "unwitting" sin. The account of Achan in Joshua 7 shows what happened to those who were guilty of premeditated seizure of things dedicated to God.

A second example of a situation that demanded a guilt offering is given in Leviticus 6:1-7. It involved anyone who may have wronged a neighbor through exploitation, robbery, fraud, or lying. When the offender becomes aware of guilt, the individual is to go and make restitution for the neighbor's loss, adding one-fifth extra to the amount of the loss, and then bring a guilt offering to be sacrificed by the priest. This example reminds us of the words of Jesus recorded in Matthew 5:23-24: "So when you are offering your gift at the altar, if you remember that your brother or sister has something against you, leave your gift there before the altar and go; first be reconciled to your brother or sister, and then come and offer your gift" (see also Luke 19:8-9).

The Ordination of the Aaronic Priests (8:1–10:20)

When Moses first spent forty days and forty nights on Mount Sinai, he received instructions for building the tabernacle and for ordaining Aaron and his sons to serve as its priests (Exod 24:15–31:18). After a delay, caused by the golden calf episode, the tabernacle was finally completed (Exod 35:1–39:43), at which time the Lord repeated the command that Aaron and his sons be ordained as priests (Exod 40:12-15). The book of Exodus ends, however, without this having been accomplished, and the story is not taken up again until we come to Leviticus 8:1–10:20. There we are given a detailed account of Israel's first ordination service, which also took place at Sinai.

The ceremony of ordination included the following elements: (1) the robing of Aaron and his sons in their priestly vesture (8:6-9); (2) the anointing with oil of the tabernacle, its furnishings, and Aaron as chief priest (8:10-12); and (3) the offering of three sacrifices, consisting of a sin offering to purify the altar (8:14-17), a burnt offering (8:18-21), and a special ordination offering (8:22-29). Part of the ceremony connected with the special ordination offering is described in 8:23. We read that after the slaying of the sacrificial ram, Moses touched some of its blood to the tip of Aaron's right ear, to the thumb of his right hand, and to the big toe of his right foot. J. H. Herz has offers this comment: "The ear was touched with blood that it may be consecrated to hear the word of God; the hand, to perform the duties of the priesthood; and the foot, to walk in the path of righteousness."[4]

The consecration and installation of Aaron and his sons as priests were climaxed by a special manifestation of the divine presence.

> Moses and Aaron entered the tent of meeting, and then came out and blessed the people; and the glory of the Lord appeared to all the people. Fire came out from the Lord and consumed the burnt offering and the fat on the altar; and when all the people saw it, they shouted and fell on their faces. (9:23-24)

The same "glory" that was present at the consecration of the tabernacle had now appeared at the consecration of the priests (see Exod 40:34-38). This had been the main purpose behind the ordination of the priests (Lev 9:6). A consecrated sanctuary would have been meaningless without a consecrated priesthood. The responsibilities of such a priesthood are summed up in Leviticus 10:10-11: "You are to distinguish between the holy and the common, and between the unclean and the clean; and you are to teach the people of Israel all the statutes that the Lord has spoken to them through Moses" (see also Mal 2:4-7).

Laws Regarding Clean and Unclean (11:1–15:33)

The book of Leviticus never gets far away from the subject of how to distinguish between the clean and the unclean, and what to do when the unclean touches you. The laws in this section were given so that the priests might teach the people how to avoid the pitfalls of the unclean. Anyone who became contaminated by contact with the unclean needed to be "detoxified" before they could fully participate in the religious life of the community.

A person's diet was a matter of deep concern to the priests, for certain living creatures were deemed to be unclean and thus unfit for human consumption. A list of the clean and unclean animals, sea creatures, birds, and insects is given in Leviticus 11:1-23, although the rationale behind the distinctions is not explained. Furthermore, the meaning of many of the Hebrew words in this list has been lost, and it is impossible to provide an accurate identification of the clean and unclean creatures. Some have even suggested that the confusion may have been intentional, and that these distinctions are binding not because they are grounded in logic, but because God ordained them. As Bailey expressed it, "This means that the regulations are to be obeyed because God wills it; that which a holy God has set aside for food is, by command, what should be eaten."[5]

It is worth noting that the New Testament allows for a greater diversity of opinion regarding clean and unclean foods. At the Jerusalem conference (Acts 15) it was agreed that Gentile believers were not bound by the food regulations of the Hebrew Scriptures, except that they should refrain from eating blood or anything killed by strangulation (Acts 15:20). Jesus taught that what entered a person's mouth could not defile, but only evil thoughts and intentions that came out of the heart (Mark 7:17-23). Mark's comment is that by saying this Jesus "declared all foods clean" (v. 19b). Paul accepted this ruling, as indicated by Romans 14:14a, "I know and am persuaded in the Lord Jesus that nothing is unclean in itself." Paul went on to add this qualifying word, however: "But it is unclean for anyone who thinks it unclean." He issued this word of warning to those who thought like he did on these matters,

> Do not, for the sake of food, destroy the work of God. Everything is indeed clean, but it is wrong for you to make others fall by what you eat; it is good not to eat meat or drink wine or do anything that makes your brother or sister stumble. (Rom 14:20-21; see also 1 Cor 8:8-13)

The bottom line for Christians in all these matters is freedom, but freedom governed by love.

Another example of ritual uncleanness that concerned the priests had to do with a woman's loss of blood at the period of menstruation or at childbirth (Lev 12). Either of these occurrences rendered her "ceremonially unclean" (v. 2) and, thus, forbidden to touch anything that was sacred or to enter the place of worship (12:4). After childbirth she was required to go through an initial purification period lasting seven days for a male child (vv. 2-3) and fourteen days for a female child. This was followed by a period of "blood purification" (v. 4), lasting thirty-three days for a male child and sixty-six days for a female child (v. 5). When the days of her purification were completed, she was supposed to bring to the priest a lamb for a burnt offering and either a pigeon or a turtledove for a sin offering (12:6). Anyone who could not afford a lamb was permitted to bring two turtledoves or two pigeons (12:8; see Luke 2:21-24).

The priests were also concerned with the ritual defilement of persons having skin diseases (13:1-14:57) or experiencing certain bodily discharges (15:1-33). The tendency among translators across the centuries has been to render the Hebrew word *tzara't* as "leprosy," even when it refers to the discoloring in the walls of houses (Lev 14:33-57). Most scholars today are convinced that it includes other skin diseases besides leprosy, such as, for example, itch and psoriasis.[6]

The Day of Atonement (16:1-34)

The Day of Atonement, known by its Hebrew title as *Yom Kippur*, falls on the tenth day of the seventh month in the Jewish calendar, corresponding approximately to our September (16:29). Its purpose was to make atonement annually for the sins of the people of Israel (16:34). This was the only occasion during the year when the high priest entered the holy of holies, there to offer the blood of the atonement sacrifices at the mercy seat (16:11-15).

A unique feature of the Day of Atonement had to do with the two goats that the people presented as their sin offering (16:5). Lots were cast at the entrance to the tent of meeting, by means of which one of the goats was chosen for the Lord and one for Azazel (16:7-8). Azazel was interpreted as the demonic ruler of the desert wastelands. The goat chosen for the Lord was sacrificed as a sin offering, with its blood used to purge the sanctuary and its altar from all the defilement caused by the sins of the people (16:15-19).

The fate of the second goat, the one chosen for Azazel, was unique to this occasion. The collective sins of the community were symbolically transferred to this goat as Aaron placed his hands on its head and confessed over it all the wrongdoings of the people. The goat was then led away into the wilderness and turned loose (16:21-22). Apparently the expectation was that Azazel would claim it. In later years it became customary to have someone push the goat off a precipice in the wilderness, in order to insure its death. Our word "scapegoat" is derived from this ancient ceremony. "Scapegoat" originated in an Old English version that referred to the second goat as "the escaping goat."

Although the Bible teaches that sacrifices alone cannot atone for sins, pious Jews came to believe that sincere repentance and the confession of sins on the Day of Atonement could make up for this deficiency. At least once a year, they believed, the slate could be wiped clean, as the sins of the people were borne away into the far reaches of the desert (16:30, 34).

The Holiness Code (17:1–26:46)

This important block of material in the last part of Leviticus is widely regarded as having originated in priestly circles near the time of the Babylonian exile, although older materials are included within it. It bears close similarities to the book of Ezekiel (see Ezek 40–48). It has come to be known as the Holiness Code because of the oft-repeated exhortation: "You shall be holy, for I the Lord your God am holy" (19:2; see also 20:7, 26; 21:6-8; 22:2, 31-33). These chapters provide a blueprint for holy living, for priests and others alike.

Some of the outstanding features of this code may be noted. One is its strong condemnation of illicit sexual behavior (18:6-30; 20:10-21). Another is its insistence upon moral rectitude and ritual correctness on the part of the priests (17:1–18:5; 21:1–22:33; 24:1-9). This code repeats the calendar of religious festivals and the instructions for their observance (23:1-14; see also Exod 23:14-17; 34:19-24). The sabbatical year and year of jubilee are treated in chapter 25.

Any discussion of the Holiness Code would be incomplete without mentioning its concern for the well-being and protection of the weaker members of society. In this respect, it reflects the prophetic demand for justice and mercy in all of life's relationships. Fair treatment is demanded for daily wage earners (19:13) and handicapped persons (19:14). Judges are commanded to be just and impartial (19:15). Merchants are told that they must use honest weights and measurements (19:35-36). Stealing, false dealing, and lying are ruled out for all of God's people (19:11).

All of these admonitions are summed up in 19:18: "You shall love your neighbor as yourself." Jesus cited this as the second most important commandment (Matt 22:39). While neighbor in this context probably refers to fellow Israelites, the Holiness Code does not stop here. Leviticus 19:34 issues the same command with respect to aliens residing among the Israelites: "The alien who resides with you shall be to you as the citizen among you; you shall love the alien as yourself, for you were aliens in the land of Egypt: I am the Lord your God." This is a commandment that we might do well to ponder at this juncture in our national history.

The Holiness Code concludes with a combination of promises and warnings (Lev 26; see also Deut 27–28). God offers the Israelites life and good fortune if they are obedient (Lev 26:3-13) but misfortune, exile, and death if they rebel (26:14-39). Even in a case where exile should occur, however, the door to restoration and forgiveness is open to those who will repent and turn back to God (26:40-45). Such is another example of a grace that is greater than all our sins.

Conclusion

Our study of covenant and law has introduced us to the Book of the Covenant and to much of the priestly legislation in the book of Leviticus. Other miscellaneous collections of priestly materials are found in Leviticus 27 and Numbers 1:1–10:10; 15; 18:1–19:22; 28:1–30:16; and 34:1–36:13. The remaining chapter of this study will examine the narrative materials scattered throughout Numbers 10:11–33:56, as well as the Mosaic materials found in the book of Deuteronomy.

It would be appropriate to conclude our study of the priestly legislation in the Pentateuch with the Aaronic blessing from Numbers 6:24-26:

> *The Lord bless you and keep you;*
> *the Lord make his face to shine upon you,*
> *and be gracious to you;*
> *the Lord lift up his countenance upon you,*
> *and give you peace.*

Notes

[1] Terrence E. Fretheim, *Exodus* (Louisville KY: John Knox Press, 1991) 247.

[2] Baruch A. Levine, "The Book of Leviticus," in *The Anchor Bible Dictionary* (New York: Doubleday, 1992) 4:312.

[3] Lloyd R. Bailey, *Leviticus* (Atlanta: John Knox Press, 1987) 33.

[4] Quoted by Bernard J. Bamberger, "Leviticus," in *The Torah, A Modern Commentary* (New York: Union of American Hebrew Congregations, 1979) 3:84.

[5] Bailey, 60.

[6] See Bamberger, 115-17.

Chapter 7

From Sinai to the Plains of Moab

Numbers 10:11–Deuteronomy 34:12

After almost a year's stay at Sinai, the Israelites set out to complete their journey to the land of Canaan (Num 10:11-12). They organized their march in accord with the instructions given in Numbers 2:1-31 (see 10:14-24). After traveling for about a month, they arrived at Kadesh-barnea, an oasis camp on the border between the wilderness of Paran and the wilderness of Zin (Num 20:1). It was from this spot that spies were later sent to scout out the land of Canaan and bring back a report (Num 13:1-3, 25-26). Because of the unfortunate outcome of this undertaking, the Israelites were condemned to spend the next forty years wandering in the wilderness around Kadesh (Num 14:26-35). It was almost as if they were "frozen in time and space," as they waited for an entire generation to die.

Events from Sinai to Kadesh

The journey from Sinai to Kadesh led the Israelites through one of the most inhospitable regions on the face of the earth. The difficulties of desert travel were brought home to me as I made a trip from Beersheba to Eilat in the summer of 1966. Much of our route lay below sea level, and the temperature had reached 100 degrees by midmorning. Several miles below Beersheba, we came upon a lone restaurant beside the road and stopped for refreshments. As we entered the restaurant, we were greeted by a chalkboard bearing a handwritten sign. It read: "You are in the Negev desert. Little water. Little electricity. Bad transportation. Unskilled staff. Little food. Always plenty of trouble. Please think of all this before you complain!"

The Israelites encountered problems even greater than those of the roadside restaurant, and there was no way to keep them from complaining. As we study this section of the book of Numbers, we have a distinct sense of *déjà vu*. It sounds like a rerun of the events described in Exodus 15:22–18:27, events that transpired on the Israelites' initial journey from the Red Sea to Sinai. Some of the duplicated experiences are God's sending of manna and quail (Exod 16; Num 11), the appointment of able leaders to assist Moses in his administrative responsibilities (Exod 18:13-26; Num 11:16-17, 24-30), and water issuing from a rock (Exod 17:1-7; Num 20:1-13). In both settings food and water were supplied to the people in response to their endless murmuring and complaining.

Psalm 78:17-22 offers the following commentary on Israel's rebellion in the wilderness:

> Yet they sinned still more against [God], rebelling against the Most High in the desert. They tested God in their heart by demanding the food they craved. They spoke against God, saying, "Can God spread a table in the wilderness? Even though he struck the rock so that water gushed out and torrents overflowed, can he also give bread, or provide meat for his people?" Therefore, when the Lord heard, he was full of rage; a fire was kindled against Jacob, his] anger mounted against Israel, because they had no faith in God, and did not trust his saving power.

The Revolt Against Moses' Authority (Num 12)

Numbers 12 recounts a story of sibling rivalry involving Aaron and Miriam against Moses. The Lord punished Miriam severely for her part in challenging the authority of Moses, but Aaron seems to have gotten off with only a mild rebuke (12:5-9). Aaron may have participated in the revolt out of a sense of jealously that God had chosen Moses instead of himself. After all, Aaron was the older of the two, and the culture in which he lived favored firstborn sons. Furthermore, Aaron had received ordination as Israel's first high priest, which may have been a further reason for him to resent the authority that Moses had assumed. Of course, we all know that jealousy among religious leaders is not something that was limited to the family of Moses.

A second cause of the friction was Moses' marriage to a black woman, a Cushite (12:1). Miriam's punishment was designed to teach her an important lesson. Since she had objected to her brother's marriage to a black woman, God determined to make Miriam "as white as snow"— with leprosy (12:10)! It was as if God were saying, "I will let you experience what it is like to be drained of all color!" One of the worst things that happens to racially prejudiced persons is that they are cut off from the stimulus and enrichment that come from contact with creative persons of other races. Whether we realize it or not, our prejudice can result in a curse, a form of social and spiritual leprosy. Like Miriam, we too can be "shut out of the camp" (12:14), forced to live in a kind of self-imposed exile. It was only Moses' intercession that saved Miriam from lifelong leprosy (12:11-15).

Rebellious Spies (Num 13–14)

Some time after the Israelites arrived at the oasis camp of Kadesh (Num 13:26), they selected twelve men, one from each of the twelve tribes, and sent them to gather intelligence about the land of Canaan. They were to report on the number and strength of the inhabitants, the condition of the soil, the kind of crops it produced, and the military preparedness of the people (13:17-20).

The mission of the spies lasted for forty days. When they returned to Kadesh, they gave conflicting reports about what they had seen. The majority reported that they had found it to be a land "flowing with milk and honey," and they displayed specimens of its fruit to prove their point (13:25-27). "However," they continued, "the people who live in the land are strong, and their cities are heavily fortified. Furthermore, we saw giants in the land, and, in comparison to them, we seemed like grasshoppers. We recommend, therefore, that we call the whole thing off. An invasion of the land could only end in death for us and our children" (see 13:28-29, 32-33). In spite of a minority report urging immediate action (13:30), fear overcame faith, and the campaign was canceled (14:1-4).

Thomas W. Mann described the tragedy of this moment in Israel's history like this:

> Numbers 13 thus presents us with what was to have been Israel's D-day, yet it proves to be a day of infamy and defeat, a day that sealed the doom of the whole wilderness generation of Israel. The reason is not difficult to find; it is the same reason that stood behind the incident of the golden calf. Israel's greatest enemy was not the Canaanite force, not even the giants among them (13:32-33); Israel's greatest enemy was the enemy within—Israel's lack of trust.[1]

After this experience the Israelites were ready to ditch Moses and Aaron, select another leader, and head back for Egypt. They preferred the security of slavery over against the risk of freedom. The generation that had come out of Egypt was unwilling to shoulder the responsibility that went with being free. For this reason, that generation must perish in the desert and make way for a new generation to arise (14:26-35). The new wine of freedom could only be stored in new wineskins. A futile attempt to reverse this judgment had disastrous consequences, and the Israelites were forced to accept their fate (14:39-45).

More Acts of Rebellion (Num 16–20)

The Israelites seem never to have learned anything from the suffering they brought upon themselves. Numbers 16 records two further instances of revolt while they were still encamped at Kadesh (see 20:22). The first instance involved Korah and a band of 250 Levites who challenged the right of Moses and Aaron to serve as priests (16:1a, 2b-11, 16-24, 35-40). The other revolt was led by Dathan and Abiram and was directed against Moses alone (10:1b-2a, 12-15, 25-34). Punishment came swiftly as the men under Korah were consumed by fire (16:35), and as Dathan and Abiram perished in what was apparently an earthquake (16:28-34).

The reaction of the people to the quelling of these two revolts was incredible. They rose up against Moses and Aaron, blaming them for the death of the rebels, to whom they referred as "the people of the Lord" (16:41-50). The Lord was ready to exterminate the people for this insolent behavior and would have done so had not Aaron offered incense upon the altar and made atonement for the people's sin (16:46-48). Even so, 14,700 of the Israelites perished in the aftermath of this rebellion (16:49).

Still, another instance of rebellion at Kadesh is recorded in Numbers 20:1-13. This is an important part of the Pentateuchal narrative, for it explains why Moses, Aaron, and Miriam were not allowed to enter the promised land. The explanation regarding Miriam is simple. She died and was buried at Kadesh (20:1). The explanation regarding Moses and Aaron is more complicated. For reasons that are not entirely clear, God was displeased with the manner in which they carried out the command to provide the people with water from the rock (20:2-13). After Moses had struck the rock twice with his rod (v. 11), God said to him and Aaron, "Because you did not trust in me, to show my holiness before the eyes of the Israelites, therefore you shall not bring this assembly into the land that I have given them" (v. 12). Shortly afterwards Aaron died and was buried on Mount Hor, at the border of Edom (20:22-29). Moses did not die until he had led the Israelites to the plains of Moab, on the eastern side of the Jordan River (Deut 34:1-8).

From Kadesh to the Plains of Moab

After mourning Aaron's death for thirty days (20:29), the Israelites headed north by way of the eastern border of Edom (21:4). Their route led across a desert area, and once again they proved that they were incurable complainers. We read that they "became impatient on the way" (21:4b). They then launched into a tirade that they had used against Moses on other occasions. They asked, "Why have you brought us up out of Egypt to die in the wilderness? For there is no food and no water, and we detest this miserable food" (21:5; see Exod 14:11-12; 17:3; Num 14:2-3; 20:4-5).

Fiery Serpents (Num 21:6-9)

Punishment for the Israelites took the form of fiery serpents (or "poisonous serpents," as in NRSV). This happened at a place called Punon (21:10; 33:43), located about twenty-five miles south of the Dead Sea. Many of the people died after being bitten by the serpents (21:6). Those who survived then repented and asked Moses to intercede for them (21:7). In response to Moses' prayer, the Lord told him to fashion a bronze serpent and to hoist it upon a pole so that anyone who had been bitten might look upon it and be healed (21:8). Moses did so, and the danger was averted (21:9).

Serpents were often regarded as symbols of healing in ancient times. Even today they are still regarded in this manner in medical circles. The account of the fiery serpent that Moses lifted up in the wilderness is also cited in John 3:14 as a symbol of the healing power of the cross of Jesus. It was an appropriate comparison, since only those who looked at the raised serpent were healed. Healing, therefore, was made available on an individual basis. Healing was conditioned upon a faith response and could be accepted or rejected. All of these factors made it an appropriate metaphor for faith in the crucified Savior.

The bronze serpent made by Moses proved to be a stumbling block to later generations of Israelites. By the time Hezekiah reigned over Judah (715–687 B.C.), a bronze serpent reputed to be that made by Moses had been placed in the Jerusalem temple and had become an object of the people's worship (2 Kgs 18:4). Hezekiah had it destroyed, along with other symbols of idolatry that had crept into Jewish religion. One generation's symbols have a way of becoming another generation's idols.

Balak and Balaam (Num 22:1–24:25)

Numbers 22:1–24:25 tells how Balak, king of Moab, was seized with fright when he saw the army of Israelites marching along the frontier of his country, and how he tried to hire Balaam to come and curse these trespassers and wipe them off the face of the earth. The curse from this renowned diviner from a distant land was to have been Balak's secret weapon against Israel. If Balaam could be persuaded to join forces with Balak, Israel's days would be numbered, or so Balak thought.

Next is a good example of Hebrew Scripture humor. According to Numbers 22:21-30, Balaam, this reputed master of blessings and curses (22:6), was actually less capable of discerning the will of God than was his donkey. The donkey not only saw the angel that Balaam could not see blocking Balaam's way (22:21-27), but the donkey carried on an extended dialogue with Balaam before the latter realized what was going on (22:28-30). After Balaam's eyes were opened (22:31), he was rebuked by the angel for the way he had mistreated his donkey (22:31-33). This passage implies that the donkey had a guardian angel watching over her, while Balaam did not. Any time a prophet has less insight than a donkey, the prophet needs to examine his or her credentials.

The oracles that Balaam was hired to speak against Israel turned out to be blessings instead of curses. There were four separate oracles, and each was profuse in its praise of Israel. For this reason, excerpts from these oracles have found their way into the ritual for certain Jewish festivals, even though the oracles were first spoken by a pagan diviner. The beginning part of Numbers 23:21, for example, has been incorporated into the liturgy for the Jewish New Year festival (Rosh Hashanah): "He [God] has not beheld misfortune in Jacob; nor has he seen trouble in Israel" (RSV). Likewise, the saying in 24:5, "How fair are your tents, O Jacob, your encampments, O Israel!" (RSV), has become a part of the liturgy to be recited as worshipers enter the synagogue.[2]

Some of the more striking tributes that Balaam paid to Israel are the following:

> How can I curse whom God has not cursed? How can I denounce those whom the Lord has not denounced? For from the top of the crags I see him, from the hills I behold him; Here is a people living alone, and not reckoning itself among the nations! Who can count the dust of Jacob, or number the dust-cloud of Israel? Let me die the death of the upright, and let my end be like his! (23:8-10)

> I see him, but not now; I behold him, but not near—a star shall come out of Jacob, and a scepter shall rise out of Israel; it shall crush the borderlands of Moab, and the territory of all the Shethites. Edom will become a possession, Seir a possession of its enemies, while Israel does valiantly. (24:17-18)

Is it any wonder that Balak felt betrayed by the one whom he had hired to curse Israel? In the end, it was Balak who was cursed and

Israel who was blessed. Having completed his task, Balaam is said to have returned to his "place" (24:25). Immediately after this, however, the men of Israel began to have sexual relations with the women of Moab and to offer sacrifices to their gods (25:1-2). Balak did not succeed in having Israel cursed, but the Israelites brought a curse upon themselves. Then, as so often in its history, Israel proved to be its own worst enemy.

The Conquest of Transjordan

After the Israelites left Kadesh en route to Canaan, they were refused passage through the territory of Edom and forced to make a tortuous detour around the eastern border of that country. The situation improved after this, however, and they were able to win a series of military victories. The first was over the king of Arad, a Canaanite city overlooking the Dead Sea, just a few miles northeast of Beersheba (21:1-3). This was a strategic victory since Arad was a formidable fortress city guarding the southern approaches to the land of Canaan. The author of this study spent two memorable days participating in the archaeological excavations going on at Arad in the summer of 1963.

The other victories of the Israelites were over Sihon, king of the Amorites (21:21-31; see Deut 1:3-4; 2:26-36), and Og, king of Bashan (21:33-35; see Deut 3:1-13a). The conquests of Sihon and Og greatly inspired the Israelites, especially in light of their previous setbacks. Psalm 136:17-22 celebrates the victory as one achieved over "great" and "famous" kings. The territories captured in these wars became Israel's first permanent possessions and the home for two and one-half of the tribes, the tribes of Gad and Reuben and the half-tribe of Manasseh (Num 32:33-42). Furthermore, these two conquests placed the Israelites on the eastern bank of the Jordan, opposite Jericho. They were within sight of their final destination! They were prepared to cross over into Canaan as soon as Moses had instructed them in the law of the Lord.

Introduction to Deuteronomy

Deuteronomy is widely considered to be the most influential book in the Pentateuch. We begin our study with a brief introduction, followed by a survey of some of the major themes of the book.

The Name

"Deuteronomy" is not a Hebrew word but a Greek word borrowed from the Septuagint's translation of Deuteronomy 17:18, where a part of the Hebrew text is rendered by the Greek phrase *deuteros nomos*, meaning "the second law." A more accurate rendering of the Hebrew of 17:18 would read "a copy of the law" (see RSV, NEB, and others). The title assigned to the book of Deuteronomy in the Hebrew Bible consists of the first two words of the Hebrew text of 1:1, translated as "these are the words." Deuteronomy, therefore, is not a "second law," but a reinterpretation of the law of Sinai designed to meet the needs of a new generation facing a new future.

The Shape

Deuteronomy is presented as a series of three farewell speeches delivered by Moses on the plains of Moab shortly before his death. The first speech (1:1–4:40) gives a review of Israel's history from the departure from Sinai until the arrival in Moab. It also appeals to the new generation of Israelites not to repeat the sins that kept their fathers and mothers from inheriting the promised land. The second speech (4:44–28:69) forms the main core of the book. It presents the basic laws of the covenant made at Sinai and warns of the dire consequences of ignoring them. The Great Commandment (6:4-5) gives a compressed summary of the entire law. The third speech (29:1–33:29) gives Moses' final exhortation and farewell to the people whom he had led for more than forty years. Chapter 34 is a concluding epilogue describing the death of Moses and giving an evaluation of his contribution to the religious life of his people. Miller has described Deuteronomy as a guide to help Israel move "from death to life (30:15-20), from slavery to freedom, from the wilderness fraught with problems to the homeland filled with promise."[3]

Influence on Other Bible Books

Deuteronomy was probably the "book of the law" discovered in the temple during the reign of Josiah (640–609 B.C.). After its discovery, it became the inspiration and blueprint for Josiah's sweeping reform of religion in seventh-century Judah (2 Kgs 22:8–23:24). Supporting evidence for this identification has been marshaled by Gottwald.[4] This would seem to indicate that Deuteronomy was likely the first of the Hebrew Scripture books to be accorded canonical recognition.

Furthermore, the historical books from Joshua through 2 Kings (not including Ruth) are currently considered to be a homogeneous grouping that has come to be known as the "Deuteronomistic History." This history traces the fortunes of the Israelites from the time they entered Canaan until they were removed to Babylon some six centuries later. Many scholars believe that the book of Deuteronomy served as the introduction and theological blueprint for this definitive work of history. This indicates the broad influence that Deuteronomy exerted on other books of the Hebrew Scriptures. It also influenced prophets such as Jeremiah and Hosea.

Deuteronomy's influence extended even to the New Testament. It is quoted a total of eighty-three times, and the quotations are found in all but six of the New Testament books. Jesus turned to Deuteronomy when he needed words with which to rebuke the tempter in the wilderness (Matt 4:4, 7, 10; see Deut 8:3; 6:13, 16). Jesus also cited Deuteronomy 6:4-5 as the greatest of all the commandments (Mark 12:28-30). Paul also drew upon Deuteronomy to reinforce his own preaching (compare 1 Cor 9:9 with Deut 25:4; Gal 3:10 with Deut 27:26).

Major Themes of Deuteronomy

Certain themes receive prominent attention in Deuteronomy. Only the major themes are presented here.

The Gift of the Good Land

Canaan was given to the Israelites in fulfillment of the promise made to Abraham centuries earlier (Gen 12:1-3). Arriving at the borders of the land was a climactic experience for Moses and the Israelites, and the significance of the occasion did not go unnoticed by the author of Deuteronomy. No book of the Bible has a richer "land theology" than this book.

Deuteronomy is especially lavish in its description of the land of Canaan. In contrast to the barren desert through which the Israelites had traveled, Canaan seemed a land "flowing with milk and honey" (6:3; 11:9; 26:9). However, Deuteronomy's favorite description of it is "a good land," a phrase that occurs some ten times in the book (see 1:25, 35; 3:25; 4:21f; and others). One of the most extravagant descriptions of the land is that found in 8:7-10, a description that begins and ends by calling it a "good land."

> For the Lord your God is bringing you into a good land, a land with flowing streams, with springs and underground waters welling up in valleys and hills, a land of wheat and barley, of vines and fig trees and pomegranates, a land of olive trees and honey, a land where you

may eat bread without scarcity, where you will lack nothing, a land whose stones are iron and from whose hills you may mine copper. You shall eat your fill and bless the Lord your God for the good land that he has given you.

The theme of thanksgiving for the gift of the land is especially prominent in 26:1-11. Verses 5b-10a contain the words the Israelites were to recite as they made a thanksgiving offering to God after their first harvest in the land of Canaan. They were to say:

A wandering Aramean was my ancestor [Jacob]; he went down into Egypt and lived there as an alien, few in number, and there he became a great nation, mighty and populous. When the Egyptians treated us harshly and afflicted us, by imposing hard labor on us, we cried to the Lord, the God of our ancestors; the Lord heard our voice and saw our affliction, our toil, and our oppression. The Lord brought us out of Egypt with a mighty hand and an outstretched arm, with a terrifying display of power and with signs and wonders; and he brought us into this place and gave us this land, a land flowing with milk and honey. So now I bring the first of the fruit of the ground that you, O Lord, have given me.

Of course, Israel's lease on this land was not guaranteed in perpetuity. The lease could be canceled if Israel violated the covenant or disregarded God's commandments (see 28:47-68). Exile from the land could also result from idolatry (4:25-26; 8:19-20; 11:16-17) or from a spirit of pride and self-sufficiency (8:11-18; 9:4-7; 28:20-21; 29:22-28).

Loss of the land was certainly not the will of the Lord for Israel. Deuteronomy is filled with practical guidelines about how this could be avoided (see 5:16, 33; 6:1-3; 11:8-9; 22:6-7; 25:13-16; 32:44-47). If Israel lost the land, which is exactly what happened in 587 B.C., it would have no one to blame but itself. The message of Deuteronomy was that even if Israel should be taken away from the land, God would still leave the door ajar for its return (4:29-31; 11:26-28; 30:1-10).

The Centralization of Worship

Deuteronomy 12:5-14 marks a turning point in the religious history of Israel. Prior to this, altars could be built and sacrifices offered in any of the places where God "caused his name to be remembered" (Exod 20:24; see also Gen 12:7; 13:18; 22:9; 26:25; 33:20). Deuteronomy 12:5 lays down a different rule; it specifies that sacrifices may be offered only at the one place among the tribes chosen to be God's habitation and the place where God's name dwells (see also 12:11, 21;

14:23, 24; 16:2, 6, 11; 26:2). This was later interpreted as referring to Jerusalem.

When the book of Deuteronomy was discovered in the Jerusalem temple in the days of Josiah (640–609 B.C.), and he became aware that sacrifices were to be permitted at only one central location, he immediately set about destroying the village altars scattered throughout the land. He also attempted to transfer to the central sanctuary in Jerusalem the Levitical priests who had previously officiated at the village altars (2 Kgs 23:8). This plan seems to have been only partially successful, for some of the country priests resisted the move to Jerusalem (2 Kgs 23:9). This decision deprived them of their livelihood, however, and the dispossessed Levites became dependent upon public charity for their support (Deut 14:27-29).

Before the village altars were destroyed, all animal slaughter was considered to be sacrificial in nature and had to be carried out by a priest. This meant that when village altars were dismantled and their priests transferred to Jerusalem, provision had to be made for the "secular" slaughtering of meat for the family table. Regulations governing such slaughter are given in Deuteronomy 12:15-25. The laws of ceremonial purification were not binding on persons partaking of meat slaughtered in this manner. The only requirement was that they not eat the blood of the slaughtered animal, but pour it out upon the ground (12:16, 23-24). Other food laws are found in Deuteronomy 14:3-21 (see Lev 11:2-23; 20:25-26).

The Demand for Justice, Mercy, and Compassion

A humanitarian spirit pervades much of the book of Deuteronomy. A splendid example of this can be found in the regulations governing the observance of the seventh year, otherwise known as the sabbatical year, or the year of release (Deut 15:1-11; see also Exod 23:10-11; Lev 25:1-7). The purpose of this observance was to turn the clock back every seven years and restore things to their original state. It was a time designed to restore liberty to Hebrew slaves (Deut 15:12-18; see Exod 21:2; Jer 34:13-16), fertility to the land (Exod 23:10-11; Lev 25:1-7), food to the poor (Deut 15:1-11; Exod 23:10-11), and real estate to its original owners (Lev 25:13-24). In other words, the people of Israel were challenged to give freedom a fresh opportunity to take root in the land. When Jesus chose a biblical model for his own ministry, it was the model of the sabbatical year (Luke 4:16-21).

Other Deuteronomic passages promoting justice, mercy, and compassion are too numerous to mention. Only a few examples can be cited. Judges were required to reject all bribes and to render just

decisions on behalf of the people (16:18-20). Kings were warned not
to acquire for themselves extravagant treasures of silver and gold or
other possessions (17:14-17). Provision was to be made for the priests
and Levites who stood to minister in the name of the Lord to be
supported by the gifts of the people (18:3-8). Anyone gathering eggs
from a bird's nest was required to let the mother bird go free (22:6).
Slaves who managed to escape were not to be returned to their owners
(23:15-16). Employers were not permitted to hold back the wages of
hired laborers, but were expected to pay the wages on the day they
were earned (24:14-15). A cloak taken as collateral for a loan was to
be returned to its owner at sunset as cover from the cold (24:10-13).
Merchants were to do business with honest weights and measures
(25:13-16). One wonders how our society would measure up to the
standards set by Deuteronomy.

The Ten Commandments
Deuteronomy 5:1-21

Before we examine the individual commandments, let us examine the
form and literary style of Pentateuchal laws. There are two classes of
Pentateuchal laws, casuistic and apodictic. Casuistic laws, otherwise
known as case laws, are thought to have originated in the context of
small tribal or village courts. Such laws usually commence with a
conditional clause, introduced by such words as "when" or "if." These
clauses present a hypothetical case involving behavior that is deemed
to be unethical, immoral, illegal, or otherwise unacceptable. This is
normally followed by a main clause detailing how the situation should
be resolved and what punishment, if any, should be administered. A
simple example of a casuistic law is found in Deuteronomy 24:7: "If
someone is caught kidnaping another Israelite, enslaving or selling the
Israelite [conditional clause], then that kidnaper shall die" [main
clause]. Other casuistic laws are found in Deuteronomy 13:6-11; 17:2-
7; and 21:18-21.

Apodictic laws are straightforward commands or prohibitions of a
categorical or unconditional nature. They express absolute and non-
negotiable demands. People do not have the option of obeying or
disobeying such laws. They are not free to determine whether the
laws are reasonable or unreasonable. Such laws are simply presented
as divine injunctions that must be obeyed. The Ten Commandments
are classic examples of apodictic laws, including both commands and
prohibitions. Other apodictic laws are rare in Deuteronomy, but may
be found in 6:4-5; 19:14; 24:17; and 25:4.

The Ten Commandments provide only the basic framework for Hebrew Scripture law. For this reason they have been referred to as policy legislation, in contrast to procedural legislation. The remaining laws of the Hebrew Scriptures are in large part an application of the principles introduced in the Ten Commandments to all areas of life, whether in the home, the courts, the marketplace, or the temple.

The First Commandment (Deut 5:6-7; Exod 20:2-3)

Deuteronomy 5:6 serves as the preamble to the entire Decalogue (another name for the Ten Commandments). It emphasizes the mighty deliverance that God wrought for Israel at the Exodus. To quote the Commandments without the preamble is to take away from their meaning. Obedience was the response of Israel to that which God had already done for its people. The yoke of the law seemed light to those who had been rescued from the yoke of Egypt.

The First Commandment decrees that the Lord alone must be Israel's God. In other words, God will not share rule with any lesser deity. God's demands are nothing short of being totalitarian when they involve the question of allegiance. James Smart has shown that we make a mockery of our religion when we picture God as willing to play second fiddle in our lives. He writes:

> Our God is a jealous God. [God] will not share the worship of our hearts with anyone or with anything; it must be concentrated upon him alone. . . . When we conceal this uncompromising claim and offer the gifts of God—the good life, forgiveness, peace with God, spiritual security—at a lesser price, we make of our church a kind of bargain counter of salvation . . . unaware that we have betrayed our people into a fatal disorder. God will not take second place.[5]

The Second Commandment (Deut 5:8-10; Exod 20:4-6)

The Second Commandment prohibits the making of any idol or image to represent the likeness of God. It is based on the principle that nothing in God's creation can fully reflect God's power and glory, much less anything that human hands have fashioned (see Jer 10:3-5, 14-16). A further rationale for rejecting idol worship is found in Deuteronomy 4:12-18. The passage teaches that since the Israelites saw no form at Sinai but only heard the sound of the Lord's voice, they had no reason to try to make an image of their God (vv. 15-18). God's revelation came through the spoken word, rather than through some visible representation. Israel's God, therefore, has no visible form, but is able to communicate through the spoken word. Idols, on the other hand, have visible forms, but are nevertheless unable to speak (see Ps 115:3-8). This fact alone is sufficient to set the religion of Israel apart from that of its pagan neighbors.

Jews later interpreted the Second Commandment as applying even to the coins they used to pay the temple tax. Since Roman coins bore the image of the emperor, they were considered unacceptable for use in the Jerusalem temple. This explains why in the days of Jesus there were money changers in the temple. They were there to assist worshipers in exchanging the forbidden Roman coins for the special Temple coins issued by the Sanhedrin.

The Third Commandment (Deut 5:11; Exod 20:7)

The New Revised Standard Version captures the broader meaning of the Third Commandment: "You shall not make wrongful use of the name of the Lord your God, for the Lord will not acquit anyone who misuses his name." The primary focus here is not upon the use of profanity, although this is certainly unbecoming to Christians, but upon the use of God's name to validate false oaths. It also applies to the use of God's name to further one's own self-interests. Lawrence Toombs has noted that this commandment is "a condemnation of any attempt to debase religion to serve one's own ends. It applies far more to the man who goes to church in order to make good business contacts than to the man who says 'O Lord!' when he hits his finger with the hammer."[6]

The Fourth Commandment (Deut 5:12-15; Exod 20:8-11)

The Sabbath is mentioned as early as Exodus 16:23 as a day on which the Israelites were not allowed to gather manna. This indicates that Sabbath observance preceded the giving of the law at Sinai.

There is a significant shift in the way the law of Sabbath observance is presented in Exodus and in Deuteronomy. Exodus speaks of the duty to keep the Sabbath as rooted and grounded in creation. Because God rested on the seventh day of creation week, Israel was to rest on the seventh day of every week. Deuteronomy, however, finds the inspiration for Sabbath observance in the Exodus event and in what God did for the Israelite slaves in Egypt. The Israelites were commanded to observe the Sabbath and keep it holy so that the persons in their households, and even the beasts that worked their fields, might have a day to rest and be refreshed from their labors. Furthermore, the Israelites were to do this as an expression of their gratitude for all that God did for them in Egypt. Because of the influence of Deuteronomy, Sabbath observance acquired a strong humanitarian emphasis in the Bible. Jesus sounded this same note when he stated that the Sabbath was made for humankind, and not humankind for the Sabbath (Mark 2:27). Miller offers this comment on the significance of the Sabbath:

> The Sabbath is a regular time to stop striving and reaching, to stop trying to justify oneself before God and everybody else; it is a time to remember having been set free and accepted in the ultimate sense and to know that the chief end of life is not found in any human work or accomplishment but only in glorifying and enjoying God.[7]

The Fifth Commandment (Deut 5:6; Exod 20:12)

The command to honor parents was not addressed primarily to young children but to adults whose parents were still living. This law was designed to prevent parents from being driven from their homes or otherwise abused when they were no longer able to work (see Exod 21:15, 17; Lev 20:9; Deut 27:16; Mark 7:9-13). Whenever the needs of senior citizens are ignored, the welfare of the nation is threatened. The promise of longevity attached to the Fifth Commandment is not so much concerned with individual longevity as with the longevity and well-being of the society that treats its older citizens with respect and dignity. This is good religion, and also good national policy.

The Sixth Commandment (Deut 5:17; Exod 20:13)

The Sixth Commandment is a prohibition against murder. This commandment has perhaps stirred up more controversy in the contemporary world than any of the other nine. The storm that has gathered around it has drawn into its vortex such issues as war, capital punishment, suicide, euthanasia, abortion, and killing in self-defense. It impinges upon such widely separated fields as religion, law, politics, medicine, and ethics.

Many are disturbed by the fact that the Bible does not forthrightly condemn war and capital punishment. Does this mean that we should accept some forms of killing as a necessary evil in a less-than-perfect world? Even if we adopt this position, we need to heed the advice of Elton Trueblood that we cultivate an uneasy conscience about the taking of human life under any circumstances. Trueblood wrote,

> If it is important to cultivate an uneasy conscience concerning the death or suffering of animals, it is a thousand times more important to cultivate such a conscience in regard to the death or suffering of human beings. It is admitted that some human beings must some-times die to save other human beings or to save a way of living

which will dignify and beautify other lives, some of them as yet unborn. All this we are forced to accept if we are reasonable and not merely sentimental, *but we dare not let ourselves get used to it and therefore treat it lightly.*[8]

The Seventh Commandment (Deut 5:18; Exod 20:14)

According to the Hebrew Scriptures, a man commits adultery by having sex with a woman who is either married or engaged to be married. Having sex with any other woman is not considered an act of adultery for a man. A married woman, on the other hand, is guilty of adultery if she has sex with anyone other than her husband, regardless of whether her sex partner is single or married. This double standard for husbands as over against wives reflects a male-dominated society.

The Bible regards monogamy, that is, the lifelong union of one man and one woman, as the norm for marriage. It also respects the sexual capacity of humans as a God-given blessing too sacred to be abused (Gen 1:28). Nothing human is more sacred or more meaningful than the love of two persons who have committed themselves to each other for life (see Song of Sol 8:6-7). The rule to be observed is that set forth in Hebrews 13:4: "Let marriage be held in honor by all, and let the marriage bed be kept undefiled; for God will judge fornicators and adulterers."

Hebrew Scripture itself is constantly revising its laws and statutes to reflect changing perspectives and changing social consciousness and circumstances. We ought, therefore, to ask whether the Seventh Commandment is not applicable also to such problems as sexual harassment, rape, spousal abuse, and pornography, especially that involving children. Modern life, with all of its complications, needs to be brought under the jurisdiction of God's Word.

The Eighth Commandment (Deut 5:19; Exod 20:15)

Some have argued that the original intent of the Eighth Commandment was to prevent the stealing of persons, or kidnapping, a crime that was punishable by death (see Exod 21:16; Deut 24:7). The Eighth Commandment, however, lists no object for the verb, and we may safely assume that it applies to all forms of theft.

The Hebrew Scriptures treat a person's goods as an extension of that person. Hence, to steal from someone is a violation of their personhood, a deliberate attempt to diminish or impoverish them. Persons whose homes have been ransacked by thieves often express the sentiment that their personal loss exceeds the value of the property that was stolen; they have been robbed of their sense of privacy and made to feel personally violated. Those who steal my purse steal more than trash; they steal a part of me!

The Ninth Commandment (Deut 5:20; Exod 20:16)

The Ninth Commandment has a legal background. A person taking the witness stand in a court of law might be either a true witness (see Prov 14:25) or a false witness (see Deut 19:16-19; Prov 14:5). The Ninth Commandment condemns the one who gives false testimony about defendants, thus robbing them of their right to a fair trial. Even malicious gossip could be classified as lying testimony against a person. The example of Naboth is a grim reminder of the damage that such testimony can cause (1 Kgs 21:1-14; see also Matt 26:59-61).

The Tenth Commandment (Deut 5:21; Exod 20:17)

The Tenth Commandment prohibits not only the subjective emotion of desiring something that belongs to your neighbor, but also the objective effort of trying to acquire the object of one's desiring. All too often a covetous spirit is the beginning of a person's downfall. Jesus taught that sometimes those who covet have already crossed the threshold of sin (Matt 5:27-28). Colossians 3:5 even equates covetousness with idolatry, that willingness to abandon God in the pursuit of some earthly goal or desire. The intent of the Tenth Commandment is to apply the brakes to human greed. Jesus once said to a young man obsessed with the fear that his brother would not give him his fair share of the family inheritance, "Take care! Be on your guard against all kinds of greed; for one's life does not consist in the abundance of possessions" (Luke 12:15).

The Great Commandment
Deuteronomy 6:4-9

The Jews have combined Deuteronomy 6:4-9 with Deuteronomy 11:13-21 and Numbers 15: 37-41 to form a prayer called the *Shema*, named after the opening word of the Hebrew text of Deuteronomy 6:4, that word being *shema*, translated "Hear!" The Jewish faithful recite this prayer twice daily, as each day begins and ends. It is also recited in times of great crisis as well as at the hour of death. No other part of the Bible is more expressive of true Jewish piety.

Deuteronomy 6:4-5 also has special significance for Christians, for Jesus referred to this as the greatest of all the commandments (Mark 12:29). This passage opens with an important affirmation about God: "Hear, O Israel: The Lord is our God, the Lord alone." *The New*

English Bible gives an alternative reading: "Hear, O Israel, the Lord is our God, one Lord." The first translation affirms that Israel's God is the only God whom Israel may worship. The second translation stresses God's undividedness, God's singularity, God's unity. Both translations are needed to express the full sense of the text: "God is *one*, and besides God there is *no other*" (see Mark 12:32-24).

The great affirmation about God is followed by a strong command (Deut 6:5). God's undividedness demands the undivided love and loyalty of God's people. It is not enough to confess that God is God alone unless the one making the confession is committed to living for God alone.

Deuteronomy 10:12-13 links the command to love God with the command for the Israelites to love other persons, in particular the widows, orphans, and aliens living among them, always remembering that they themselves had been aliens in the land of Egypt (10:16-19). Jesus followed Deuteronomy's lead in linking the two commandments to love God and to love one's neighbor as oneself (Mark 12:31). Paul also described love for one's neighbor as "the fulfilling of the law" (Rom 13:10).

The Great Commandment was of such significance that Deuteronomy sought to insure its continuing authority and influence over the people. Its words were to be kept in the heart of each Israelite (6:6). Its words were to be taught to the children in the homes of the Israelites (6:7, 20-25). No book of the Bible shows a greater concern than Deuteronomy for the transmission of the faith to the next generation (see 4:9-10; 11:18-21; 29:22-28; 31:9-13). Children were to be so lovingly taught by their parents that the children's last thoughts before falling asleep and their first thoughts upon awaking would be about the Lord's mercy and compassion (6:7).

Moses' Last Days

One of the pressing problems facing the Israelites as they waited to cross the Jordan was the selection of Moses' successor. The record of how this problem was handled is found in Numbers 27:12-23 and Deuteronomy 31:1-8, 14-15, 23. Moses began by reminding the Israelites that it would not be possible for him to cross the Jordan with them (Deut 31:1-2). He then informed them that God had chosen Joshua as his successor (31:3). Moses summoned Joshua and charged him to be strong and courageous in the fulfillment of his new responsibilities (31:7-8). Moses and Joshua then made their way to the door of the tent of meeting where God appeared and gave Joshua his commission:

"Be strong and bold, for you shall bring the Israelites into the land that I promised them; I will be with you" (31:23; see also Josh 1:7-9).

The history of Israel's sojourn in the wilderness is brought to a close shortly after this change of command. Moses ascended to the top of Mount Nebo. From there God showed him the land that the Israelites were to inherit, a good land that stretched as far as the eye could see (34:1-4). Moses then died and was buried at an undisclosed site near the foot of Mount Nebo (34:5-6). Israel had lost its greatest leader, and it was appropriate to remember Moses as the greatest prophet who ever graced the pages of that nation's history (34:10-12).

Conclusion

The Torah ends very much the way it began. Just as God placed the earth before Adam and Eve and offered it to them as their dominion, so God places the land of Canaan before Israel and offers it to them. Just as God provided for Adam and Eve a commandment, obedience to which would mean continued blessing, but disobedience to which would entail a curse, so God has blessed Israel as God's special people, but warned them of the curse that leads to death. Just as Adam and Eve could be genuinely human only in responsibility to the divine will, so Israel can be God's holy nation only in responsibility to God's torah.[9]

—Thomas W. Mann

Notes

[1]Thomas W. Mann, *The Book of the Torah* (Atlanta: John Knox Press, 1988) 131.

[2]See W. Gunther Plaut, in *The Torah, A Modern Commentary* (New York: Union of American Hebrew Congregations, 1979) 4:233, 242.

[3]Patrick D. Miller, *Deuteronomy* (Louisville KY: John Knox Press, 1990) 20.

[4]Norman K. Gottwald, *A Light to the Nations* (New York: Harper & Brothers, 1959) 334f.

[5]James D. Smart, *The Old Testament in Dialogue with Modern Man* (Philadelphia: Westminster Press, 1964) 70.

[6]Lawrence Toombs, *Nation Making* (New York and Nashville: Abingdon Press, 1962) 47.

[7]Miller, 82f.

[8]Elton Trueblood, *Foundations for Reconstruction* (New York: Harper & Brothers, 1946) 67.

[9]Mann, 161.

ALL **THE** BIBLE

ALL THE BIBLE SERIES DESCRIPTION

AREA	TITLE*
Genesis–Deuteronomy	Journey to the Land of Promise
Former Prophets	Israel's Rise and Decline
Latter Prophets, excluding Postexilic	God's Servants, the Prophets
Poetry, Wisdom Literature	The Testimony of Poets and Sages
Exilic, Postexilic Books	The Exile and Beyond
The Four Gospels	The Church's Portraits of Jesus
Acts of the Apostles, Epistles of Paul	The Church's Mission to the Gentiles
Hebrews–Revelation	The Church as a Pilgrim People

Titles Subject to Change